AS/400 Control
Language Guide

D1715461

AS/400 CONTROL LANGUAGE GUIDE

Brian Fu

A Wiley-QED Publication

JOHN WILEY & SONS, INC.
NEW YORK • CHICHESTER • BRISBANE • TORONTO • SINGAPORE

Library of Congress Cataloging-in-Publication Data

Fu, Brian.
AS/400 Control language guide / Brian Fu.
     p.   cm.
     Includes bibliographical references and index.
     ISBN 0-471-61152-2
     1. IBM AS/400 (Computer)—Programming. 2. Job Control
     Language (Computer program language).
I. Title.
QA76.8.I25919F8 1994
005.4'3—dc20   93-37543
                                                                CIP

Printed in the United States of America

10 9 8 7 6 5 4 3 2 1

Trademarks

IBM is a registered trademark of International Business Machines Corporation.

UNIX is a registered trademark of AT&T.

MS-DOS is a registered trademark of Microsoft Corporation.

AS/400, Application System/400 are registered trademarks of International Business Machines Corporation.

OS/400, is a registered trademark of International Business Machines Corporation.

Important Note

Permissions

Permission to excerpt IBM copyrighted screen images and materials has been granted by International Business Machines Corporation. These illustrations include Figures 2.1, 2.2, 2.3, 2.4, 9.2, 10.1, and 10.2.

Limits of Liability and Disclaimer or Warranty

The author makes no warranty, express or implied, with regard to the programs or the documentation contained in this book. The author shall not be liable in any event for incidental or consequential damages in connection with, or arising out of, the furnishing, performance, or use of these programs.

Contents

3   THE BASIC ELEMENTS   34

6   JOBS   97

8 MESSAGE HANDLING   156

9   FILE PROCESSING   189

Preface

This book is for systems professionals and programmers who have no or very little experience on the IBM AS/400. The control language is the vehicle of communication between the machine and the user, and it is the most important language an AS/400 user has to learn.

This book is divided into ten chapters. Each chapter contains materials that are prerequisites of the chapters that follow. Illustrations and lines of code are used to convey this knowledge more efficiently and help the readers learn more easily.

Many pages have been devoted to the basic concepts of the AS/400 system architecture. As we know, the system architecture is the foundation of the control language, it affects the characteristics of the control language, and the control language is impossible to understand without knowing the system concepts of the machine.

The author has put his best efforts into preparing this book and would welcome any comments on its contents from the readers.

Acknowledgments

This book would not exist without the generous support and assistance of the people at John Wiley and QED, and especially Edwin Kerr and Maureen Drexel.

1

The Story of the AS/400

1.1. Introduction

The subject of this book is the IBM Application System/400 Control Language (AS/400 CL). The control language is one of the most important languages on the AS/400 since it is the vehicle for communication between the user and the machine. Most of the CL programs are written to perform system tasks. We simply cannot work with the AS/400 without knowing any control language, which we will learn about in the following chapters.

In this chapter we will look at the history and some technical background of the IBM midrange family. This chapter is divided into three main parts: Section 1.2 tells you the history of the System 3X family, the predecessors of the AS/400; Section 1.3 introduces you to the basic architectural concept of the AS/400; and Section 1.4 shows you some basic system commands that can be used to get technical information about your AS/400 machine.

In this chapter, we will get a basic idea of the following:

- Object-based architecture
- Single-level storage addressing method
- Layered design of software

I do not plan to go into the details of the hardware architecture of the AS/400, they only concern computer engineers. We will cover just very basic hardware technical material.

As some computer industry observers projected, the two dominant players in the computer industry in the 1990s will be the AS/400 and the open system. The AS/400 is popular because of its integrated database, system architecture, and machine reliability. On the other hand, the major reason for the popularity of the open system is that it is not a vendor-specific operating system, and software written on any machine that runs a similar operating system would be portable to another platform. The open system is getting the attention because of its software portability and interoperability. Nevertheless, the AS/400 is still the most popular midrange computer so far and will continue to be a dominant player in the 90s.

The IBM AS/400 family of products was unveiled in June 1988. The AS/400 has very close architectural similarities with the IBM System/38, which is recognized as the predecessor of the AS/400. Since the announcement of the AS/400 family, IBM has regularly announced new models of hardware and operating system upgrades.

The AS/400 family of products is a line of mid-range computing systems based on one single software architecture. The AS/400 is a minicomputer and also a multiuser computing system, that is, a single computer serving more than one user at a time. The predecessors of AS/400 are the System/36 and System/38, and today many of the applications running on these systems can be migrated to the AS/400 system using certain migration tools.

1.2. The Predecessors of the AS/400 — System 3X

1.2.1. System/3

The first member of the IBM midrange family was the System/3.

System/3 was announced in July 1969 and was delivered in January 1970. The System/3 was designed as a punched card-oriented computer system. The marketing strategy of IBM was to use the System/3 to target the lower end of the market segment while using the mainframes to target the upper end.

There were only about 3000 logic circuits in the architecture design of the System/3 — relatively small when compared to the mainframes. The System/3 was famous for introducing the 96-column card format that could store about 20 percent more information than the traditional 80-column punched card. The System/3 was originally designed to have only 24KB memory but was expanded to 64KB later. It used the 16-bit address size, but the addressing method used by System/3 allowed the machine to extend its memory beyond the 64KB limit.

The primary customers targeted by IBM at that time were mainly commercial users running small size applications. Therefore the mode of processing on the System/3 was predominantly batch processing. In 1972, IBM added the Communications Control Program (CCP) to the System/3, which provided the interactive processing capabilities. The original intent of the CCP was to be mainly operator-oriented.

The System/3 was created for commercial use and focused on intensive data processing for the business world; therefore, in order to buy system performance as much as possible, it did not use microcode to implement its instruction set but instead was hard-wired. In 1973, the System Control Program (SCP) and Operator Control Language (OCL) were introduced to System/3 users.

Basically, the System Control Program provided support for the multiprogramming environment, printer spooling control, data management and system logging facilities and so forth. The Operator Control Language, on the other hand, became the vehicle between the user and the machine and is the ancestor of the control language.

The System/3 was quite popular for a while. However, its problem was the operational compatibility with the mainframes, and since it used the 96-column card format, which was not compatible with the 80-column card format on the mainframe, it made the migration and networking problem an issue.

1.2.2. System/32

The System/32 was announced and delivered in January 1975.

The System/3 had been designed as a small, general-purpose distributed data processing system, but the System/32 was designed as a fully integrated single-user system. The System/32 had a maximum of 32KB memory and a maximum of 27MB hard disk storage. However, the main processor was designed to assume dual roles. The first role was to execute the stored programs in main memory and the second role was to perform input/output (I/O) control functions. Since the central processor had to perform dual roles in which the number of I/O operation control functions could be quite heavy, especially in commercial applications, the System/32 was given an optimized native instruction set to perform the I/O functions and the control functions were hard-wired, similar to the System/3.

1.2.3. System/34

The System/34 was introduced in April 1977 to answer the demand for a low-cost, interactive and multiuser computer system. The System/34 was IBM's first multiuser minicomputer system.

The System/34 had a maximum of 256KB main memory and 256MB hard disk storage. It could support up to 16 local workstations and 64 remote workstations connected to the host machine. The System/34 supported interactive environment by distributing I/O workload to special processors. The main processor of the System/34 had the dual-processor design, similar to that of the System/32. The system processors included the Main Storage Processor (MSP), which was responsible for executing stored programs, and the Control Storage Processor (CSP), which took over system control and I/O operations. The System/34 had the 16-bit address size, similar to the System/3.

1.2.4. System/36

In May 1983, IBM announced the System/36. The System/36 was almost identical to the System/34 in computer architecture. It also had the dual-processor design, that is, the dual MSP/CSP design. However, it increased the address size to 24 bits and introduced 16-bit data paths, and thus could support larger memory demands and a faster data transfer rate. In addition, IBM introduced the dynamic random access memory (DRAM) technology and implemented this new technology to the System/36. DRAM technology has the densest memory in commercial use.

Since its introduction, the System/36 has been the most popular midrange machine up to the introduction of the AS/400. About 250,000 system units have been sold since 1983.

1.2.5. System/38

Although 38 numerically follows 36, the System/38 actually was born before the System/36.

In October 1978, the System/38 was introduced. There were some revolutionary ideas in the architectural design of the System/38. System/38 was the first computer to employ the design concept of single-level addressability of storage, which treats all types of physical storage on the machine as if they are in one vast region in the main memory. Of course, single-level addressability of storage must be supported by very large virtual address space. The System/38 was the first machine ever constructed using the concept of single-level addressability of storage.

In addition to that, System/38 also employed the new concept of layered design in architecture, which isolates machine hardware and system software through a series of horizontal interfaces. The System/38 operating system (called the Control Program Facility, or CPF) was designed to execute on a "logical" computer rather than on a physical computer so that any object on the system is referenced by its name rather than by its location. The functions of this "logical" computer were defined by the machine interface (MI). The MI was implemented by microcode on the System/38 hardware. The advantage of this layered design is that the low-level functions can be replaced by improved technology at any time yet cause minimal disruption to the high-level system software, since the system software and hardware are already separate.

Another new concept introduced to the System/38 is the object-based architecture. This object-based concept is still employed and implemented on the AS/400 architecture.

The object-based architecture was first discussed and implemented in database and software analysis and design in the late 1980s. However, the System/38 and AS/400 are the first machines to have employed the concept of object-based in its operating system design.

Object-based architecture means that every stored entity on the system, no matter whether it is a program, a file, or a user profile, is referenced by its name rather than by its location. This is also called the "capability-based addressing method." Whenever the system needs to locate an object to perform an action on the named object, the system will automatically verify that the requested action to be performed is valid on the requested object. This is to make sure that any action to be performed is qualified for the object. By the same token, the system can also synchronize access to the same object and thus enhance data integrity and system security.

1.3. The Arrival of the AS/400

The Application System/400 was announced and delivered in June 1988.

The AS/400 family consists of three basic computers: the 9402, 9404, and 9406 systems. The 9402 systems consist of two models, the C04 and C06, and are the smallest in the family in terms of horsepower when compared with the other models in the AS/400 family. When the original AS/400 family was introduced, the 9404 systems consisted of the models B10 and B20. They have been replaced by the more powerful C10, C20, and C25 models. The 9406 systems make up the larger end of the family and include the most powerful AS/400 computers. They have higher performance, can support more communication lines, and have more storage. They have greater expandability than the 9402 and 9404 models as well. Originally, there were four AS/400 systems in the 9406 series: B30, B40, B50, and B60. Later the models B35, B45, and B70 were added to the series.

The AS/400 system hardware includes the processor and main storage, the I/O devices and controllers, and the racks, cables, and connectors. At the center of the AS/400 is the system unit, which includes the following:

- System processor (CPU)
- Main storage
- Cache memory, if any
- Multifunction I/O processors, which include storage I/O processor, workstation I/O processor, and communication I/O processor
- Fixed disk
- Diskette, tape, or cartridge unit

Peripherals such as printers, terminals, and workstations are connected to the system unit with twinaxial cable. The maximum number of terminals and workstations that can be connected to the system unit depends on the maximum number of communication lines, twinaxial workstation controllers, and ASCII workstation controllers allowed. The maximum number of the communication lines and controllers depend in turn on the model of the system unit.

System components such as additional racks, I/O controllers, and storage and workstation devices can be added incrementally without reconfiguring the whole system.

Figure 1.1 shows the AS/400 system hardware architecture.

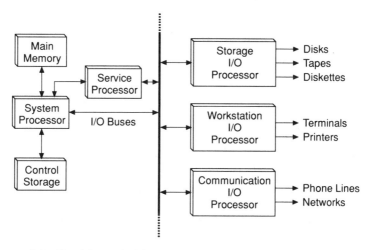

Figure 1.1. The AS/400 hardware architecture.

The AS/400 system is designed around the system bus I/O architecture, which connects the I/O processors to the system processor. The design consists of the separate control processors, which
include multifunction I/O processors, for instance, the storage I/O
processor, the workstation I/O processor, and the communication
I/O processor as well as the system processor. The benefit of this
design is that the workload in input/output operations for the central
system processor is reduced and delegated to the separate control
processors so that the system processor can now dedicate more of its
resources to other non-I/O tasks. An I/O processor communicates
with the system processor and controls the devices attached to it. The
number of system processors varies and depends on the model of the
machine. Models D90, D95, E90 and E95 have more than one processor; these are called "N-way" processor architecture. This architecture provides flexibility for future growth by allowing the addition of multiple processors. Additional processors are transparent to
the users since they share the workload evenly among the processors.

Figure 1.2 shows an AS/400 network scenario, in which one
single AS/400 machine is supporting several terminals through
twinaxial cables. PCs can be attached to the AS/400 machine either
as a Programmable Workstation (PWS) or a dumb terminal. If the
PC is supported by the AS/400 through an emulation software pack-
age, the AS/400 treats the PC as a dumb terminal.

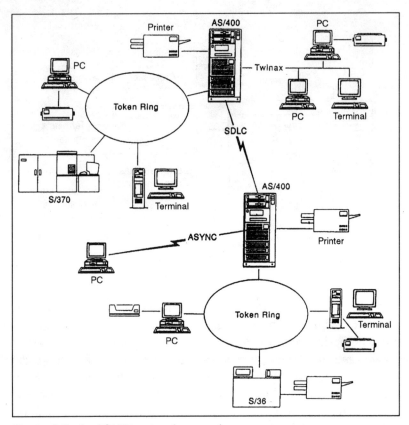

Figure 1.2. An AS/400 network scenario.

In some hardware configurations the AS/400 can be used as a server, but in some others they are used as a client. For example, the AS/400 in our illustration is used as a server and the PCs and the workstations used as clients, but in some larger configurations the mainframe is used as a server and the AS/400 is used as a client. The client/server relationship describes the way the information and resources are shared. The server in a client/server environment is the owner of the data and has the database update capability, on the other hand, the client in a client/server environment is the user of the data.

The figure also shows that two AS/400 machines are connected. Data and programs on both machines can be shared by users on both machines through a communication line. There are several types of physical connections that can be used to link the AS/400 with the other machines in the network.

The AS/400 system has a layered design of its software, as mentioned above, originating from the layered design concept of the System/38.

Figure 1.3 shows the layers of software on the AS/400.

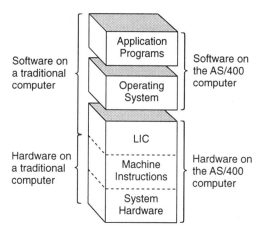

Figure 1.3. AS/400 layered design of software.

The top layer of the software is the application programs. They are the HLL programs written by the users to perform daily business applications, for example, accounting, order entry, manufacturing, scheduling, and so forth. The other layers below it are providing support to the application layer.

The next layer below the application programs is called the operating system. The operating system performs the detailed house-keeping tasks associated with the internal workings of the computer and provides the environment in which the application programs can execute.

The next layer below the operating system is called the LIC (Licensed Internal Code) layer. The LIC is actually a set of programs provided by IBM. These programs are always being invoked by other programs in the application programs layer or the operating system layer to do specific tasks, and they would never interact with the users directly. LIC also isolates the application programs from the hardware and thus allows for hardware improvements without hindering the application programs' compatibility. It is the LIC layer that makes the AS/400 computer different from traditional computers.

The built-in database capacity, single-level storage addressing method, and object-oriented operating system are all implemented into the LIC layer, making them part of the machine hardware. The advantage of this design is improved efficiency and system performance.

Tip

Many functions that are traditionally performed by system control programs are integrated into the LIC on the AS/400, thus resulting in a more efficient system.

In April 1991, IBM announced 11 new models of the AS/400. The AS/400 models C4 through B70 have been replaced by models prefaced with the letter D. The D models outperform their B and C counterparts by up to 60 percent. The new D models not only have faster processors, but also have newer and faster tape devices and controllers, and a new direct access storage device (DASD) and tape drive.

The model D80 is also the first model to have the N-way processor, which has dual processors that can do work concurrently, thus making it faster to get the same task done. All 9406 D models have 1.2GB internal DASD and a five-minute battery backup unit; in the event of a disaster the system memory dumps to the internal DASD to allow for a fast re-IPL. Models D50 and later use fiber-optic cables to connect the racks, which improves the data transfer rate. The new Token Ring local area network (LAN) adapter, combined with the improved operating system, increases the AS/400's capabilities as a server in a client/server environment.

In February 1992, IBM again completely replaced the AS/400 product line and announced the entirely new E model series. Within this new product line, the lower-end models are very competitive with any leading PC local area network system, and those of the upper end can match a mainframe computer. It is IBM's intention to make the AS/400 a "full range" product. The top of the range is the Model E90, which has a 3-way processor. That is, three separate processors are linked to perform concurrent tasks, thus improving system performance. Actually, in the model D series, IBM has already introduced the D80, which has the dual-processors design. Since then, IBM has increased the use of the N-way processors concept.

In September 1992, IBM announced the new release of an operating system and the new Model E95. The new Model E95 fea-

tures a four-way processor, which actually is four separate processors linked together to accomplish concurrent tasks. IBM declared
that the new Model E95 has a 20 percent increase in performance
over that of Model E90. The Model E95 is positioned as a logical
replacement of the mainframe 43XX and 3080 models. For compa-
nies considering "downsizing," AS/400 with expanded memories
offers a cost-effective alternative to the mainframes.

In February 1993, IBM announced the 14-member F series
family. The new series has improved input/output function and cli-
ent/server capabilities. The F80, F90, and F95 use two, three, and
four coupled system processors integrated through N-way multipro-
cessor architecture. The F series uses new technologies to provide
25 to 60 percent more throughput than their predecessors. The models F70 through F95 employ the first use of bi-CMOS (bipolar
complementary metal-oxide semiconductor) logic together with
multichip modules that replace the entire controller boards. The F
series supports more workstation controllers, and the top-of-the-line
F95 gives 10 times as much throughput as the AS/400 had when it
was first introduced in 1988. The F95 has reached the horsepower of
the mainframe in terms of system performance, and the new AS/400
models overall can grow to support more users and more complex
applications.

In summary, the strengths of the AS/400 include the following:

1. The operating system provides a comprehensive, fully integrated set of batch and interactive work management functions that make processing application programs efficient
   and productive.
2. It has the built-in data management functions that provide a
   full range of data description capabilities and a consistent
   interface for access to data.
3. All data can reside in a single, integrated relational database, with query functions that make information readily
   available.

1.4. Know Your AS/400

We have completed the short history of the IBM 3X/400 family.

You can work with the hardware configurations of your machine by using the following very basic CL commands:

1. Work with System Status (WRKSYSSTS)

2. Work with Configuration Status (WRKCFGSTS)
3. Work with Disk Status (WRKDSKSTS)

1.4.1. Work with System Status

The Work with System Status (WRKSYSSTS) command lets you
work with the information about the current status of the system,
which is primarily about main and auxiliary storage information. You
would definitely need this command in performance tuning. Figure
1.4 shows the display upon calling WRKSYSSTS. You can press the
function key <F11> to display some other statistics for each pool.
Information included in the WRKSYSSTS display includes:

- Number of jobs currently on the system
- Capacity of auxiliary storage
- Percentage of system storage in use
- Amount of temporary storage in use
- Percentage of machine addresses used
- Statistical information about each storage pool

```
                        Work with System Status              BRIAN
                                              09/29/92   14:13:33
% CPU used . . . . . . . :      98.0   Auxiliary storage:
Elapsed time . . . . . . :   00:00:00      System . . . . . . . . :    18877 M
Jobs in system . . . . . :       231   % used . . . . . . . . :    89.5253
% addresses used:                          Total  . . . . . . . . :    18877 M
    Permanent  . . . . . . :   25.312   Current unprotect used :      609 M
    Temporary  . . . . . . :    3.811   Maximum unprotect  . . :      617 M

Type changes (if allowed), press Enter.

System    Pool   Reserved    Max   -----DB-----   ---Non-DB---
 Pool   Size (K) Size (K)  Active  Fault  Pages   Fault  Pages
   1     18930     8759     +++     .0     .0      .0    43.4
   2      8722        0      5      .0     .0     21.7   43.4
   3       319        0      5      .0     .0      .0     .0
   4      6144        0      3      .0   217.3    43.4   43.4
   5     64189        0     30      .0     .0      .0     .0
                                                              Bottom

===>
F3=Exit    F4=Prompt           F5=Refresh   F9=Retrieve   F10=Restart
F11=Display transition data    F12=Cancel   F24=More keys
```

Figure 1.4. Work with System Status display.

In the pool size column in Figure 1.4, you can see that the main
storage of this AS/400 has been divided into five system storage
pools. The summation of the individual pool size should give you
the total size of the main storage for your AS/400 machine:

```
(18,930 + 8,722 + 319 + 6,144 + 64,189) KB = 98 MB
```

So, the main storage of this AS/400 has the size of 98 MB, approximately. The main storage of the AS/400 is divided into storage pools, which are logical segments of main storage. This will reduce the amount of interference among jobs competing for main storage and can prevent a large job from using too much main storage. However, a storage pool is not necessarily a contiguous partition of main storage. Instead, it is 1 KB increments of main storage that are available. These increments can be anywhere in main storage.

Also from the figure above, we can see that this AS/400 has total DASD space of 18 GB, in which 89.5 percent is already allocated. In most situations, when the DASD usage has reached 85 percent or above, the system performance starts to degrade.

Tip

Use the statistics in the WRKSYSSTS command to allocate spaces for each storage pool in performance tuning.

1.4.2. Work with Configuration Status

The Work with Configuration Status (WRKCFGSTS) command lets you work with the configuration elements and their current status on the system. The WRKCFGSTS command displays the status information for communication lines, controllers, devices, network interfaces (if your AS/400 is connected to a network), and any jobs associated with these devices. Configuration descriptions are displayed for the line, controller, or device selected.

1.4.3. Work with Disk Status

The Work with Disk Status (WRKDSKSTS) command lets you work with the disk activity statistics and storage level. The display in Figure 1.5 shows you the disk activity level. The last column is the % Busy statistics, and it is a very useful figure since it shows you whether the disk unit has been overworked. If the % Busy figure exceeded 40 percent, you would probably experience a serious response time problem.

```
                          Work with Disk Status
Elapsed time:    00:01:28

          Size    %     I/O   Request  Read  Write  Read  Write   %
Unit  Type  (M)  Used   Rqs   Size (K)  Rqs   Rqs   (K)   (K)   Busy
  1   2800  320  62.2   .1     1.2      .1    .0    .6    2.8    0
  2   2800  320  31.5   .0      .0      .0    .0    .0    .0     0
  3   2800  320  30.6   .0      .0      .0    .0    .0    .0     0
  4   2800  320  30.5   .0     2.1      .0    .0   2.1    .0     0
  5   9336  857  29.6   .2     1.7      .1    .0   1.9    .5     0
  6   9336  857  29.6   2.6    1.3     2.5    .0   1.1   11.8    5
  7   9336  857  29.6   .0      .5      .0    .0    .0    .5     0
  8   9336  857  29.6   .1      .5      .0    .1   1.0    .5     0




                                                           Bottom
Command
===>
F3=Exit   F5=Refresh   F12=Cancel   F24=More keys
```

Figure 1.5. Work with Disk Status display (disk activity level).

1.4.4. System Values

Besides the three "Work with" commands above, you can also use the Display System Values (DSPSYSVAL) command to find out the other general system information of your AS/400. For example, to find out the model of your AS/400, you can use the DSPSYSVAL command:

```
DSPSYSVAL SYSVAL(QMODEL)
```

The DSPSYSVAL command shows you the information online. There are about 70 system values that control the operations of your AS/400.

Tip

Use the DSPSYSVAL command to display the system values online.

Command Summary

WRKSYSSTS	Work with System Status
WRKCFGSTS	Work with Configuration Status
WRKDSKSTS	Work with Disk Status
DSPSYSVAL	Display System Values

Exercises

1.1. Explain the following terms:
Object-based operating system
Single-level addressing method
Layered design of software

1.2. What are the strengths of the AS/400?

1.3. Briefly describe the kinds of information you would get by using the following commands:
Work with System Status (WRKSYSSTS)
Work with Configuration Status (WRKCFGSTS)
Work with Disk Status (WRKDSKSTS)

1.4. Find out what kinds of controlling parameters are stored as system values.

2

An Introductory Tutorial

This chapter is divided into two parts: basic terms and concepts, and the tutorial exercise.

The purpose of this chapter is to give the readers some hands-on experience using the AS/400. However, there are several terms and basic concepts that you need to understand fully before you do any of these tutorial exercises. These basic concepts will also lead you to the remaining chapters of this book.

The tutorial exercise in Section 2.2 will introduce you to a set of commands you will use frequently as an AS/400 user or programmer.

2.1. Basic Terms and Concepts

2.1.1. Control Language

Control language is the set of system commands with which the user makes a request to the system to perform the required function.

A control language (CL) program is a sequence of control language commands running by batch. CL programs provide a vehicle for communication between the user and the machine.

The basic elements of a CL program include the control language command and the program construct that organizes these commands into meaningful structures. There are over 700 CL commands on the AS/400. Most of these CL commands can be run directly at the system command line interactively, or they can be invoked from the AS/400 menus, and some of them can be coded into source file and compiled into a program.

2.1.2. Object

An object must have a name and occupy storage space. On the AS/400 system, a wide variety of entities are objects — files, libraries, folders, programs, user profiles, queues, subsystems, and command definitions, and so forth.

Each object is identified by its object name and object type.

The object name is explicitly assigned by the system for system objects or by the user when creating the object.

The object type is detemined by the command that created the object. Each type of object has a unique purpose within the system. Different object types have different operational characteristics and each has an associated set of commands with which to process that type of object.

The AS/400 is said to be an object-based machine. The object-based concept states that every stored entity on the system is referenced by its name rather than by its location. This is also called the "capability-based addressing method." Whenever the system needs to locate an object to perform an action, the system will automatically verify that the requested action to be performed is valid on the requested object. This is to make sure that any action to be performed is qualified for the object.

An object has a set of characteristics that describe itself; this set of attributes is called the object descriptions. The information includes the object name, library name, object type, object size, created date and time, user who created the object, user who owns the object, date last used, storage size, and so forth.

The object authority controls what a system user can do with the object. The object authority includes deleting, moving, or renaming the object. There are three types of object authorities: object operational, object management, and object existence.

Each object is owned by its object owner.

With this object-based orientation, every object is handled in a consistent manner. The system recognizes each object by its type, which determines how it can be used.

2.1.3. Library

A library is an object that serves as a directory to other objects. It is a way of organizing objects on the AS/400 system. A library groups related objects and allows the user to locate an object by its object name. A library itself is an object. However, on the AS/400 each library is independent of each other and there are no hierarchies among the libraries, so the library organization is very different from the file system structure.

A library list is a list that indicates which libraries are to be searched and the order in which they are to be searched for an object. The system searches through the whole library list to find the named object in the order of occurrence until an object with the same name and type is found. If there is more than one object having the same name and type in these libraries, you would always get the object that the system finds first. One thing you should bear in mind is that if the library that contains the expected object is not in the library list, the system will not be able to find the object even though it really exists. Thus, it is very important that the library is added to the library list before you run the program that would look for the object.

2.1.4. Job

A job is a single, identifiable sequence of processing actions that represent a single use of the system. Therefore, every piece of work that runs in a subsystem is called a job. The two major types of jobs on the AS/400 are interactive and batch.

2.1.4.1. Interactive Job

An interactive job starts when someone signs on to a workstation and ends when the user signs off from the system.

2.1.4.2. Batch Job

A batch job is a predefined sequence of processes submitted to a job queue to be performed without any interactions from the user. Opposite of interactive jobs.

2.1.5. Job Queue

Job queue is an object that contains a list of batch jobs waiting to be processed.

2.1.6. Subsystem

A subsystem is a single, predefined operating environment in which the system coordinates the work flow and resource. You can always create a subsystem whose attributes determine how work is to be done under that particular environment, and you can always run a job under that environment after it is defined. The subsystem is defined by a subsystem description. The subsystem description contains information defining how the operating environment will be controlled by the system, and the way resources and processes are to be coordinated.

2.1.7. Output Queue

An output queue is the place to store the output files produced by a program.

2.1.8. Message Queue

The message queue is the place to store the messages sent between users, between jobs, between programs, between user and program, and so forth.

2.2. Introductory Tutorial

This section will give you some hands-on experience in editing and compiling a CL program and calling some basic commands.

2.2.1. First Things First

To start the tutorial, the first thing you need to do is to sign on to the AS/400. You can see the standard sign-on screen as shipped by IBM in Figure 2.1.

Enter your user profile and the password. A password may be required depending on the security level of your AS/400.

```
                        Sign On

                                   System  . . . . . :   BRIAN
                                   Subsystem . . . . :    QINTER
                                   Display . . . . . :    DSP01

          User  . . . . . . . . . . . . . ._____
          Password  . . . . . . . . . . . .
          Program/procedure . . . . . . . ._____
          Menu  . . . . . . . . . . . . . ._____
          Current library . . . . . . . . ._____




                        (C) COPYRIGHT IBM CORP. 1980, 1991.
```

Figure 2.1. AS/400 sign-on screen.

A user profile is an object with a unique name that contains the user's password, the list of special authorities, and the objects the user owns. The user profile cannot be longer than 10 characters in length and it may include alphabets and digits. The minimum and maximum length of the user profile and the minimum number of digits required are determined by the system.

Let's look at the standard sign-on screen in Figure 2.1 in more detail.

1. System is the name you gave to your AS/400.
2. Subsystem is the environment you set up for interactive jobs.
3. Display is the device name of your workstation.

Below the user profile and the password there are three other entries on the screen.

1. Program/procedure is the program you want to run after your sign-on has become successful.
2. Menu is the menu you want the system to load after you login to the system.
3. You can specify the current library at the current library entry.

The current library is the first user library to be searched for objects requested by the user. The current library is also the library that the system uses when a new object is created.

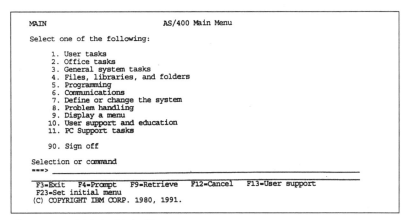

```
MAIN                        AS/400 Main Menu

Select one of the following:

     1. User tasks
     2. Office tasks
     3. General system tasks
     4. Files, libraries, and folders
     5. Programming
     6. Communications
     7. Define or change the system
     8. Problem handling
     9. Display a menu
    10. User support and education
    11. PC Support tasks

    90. Sign off

Selection or command
===>
_____
 F3=Exit    F4=Prompt    F9=Retrieve    F12=Cancel    F13=User support
 F23=Set initial menu
 (C) COPYRIGHT IBM CORP. 1980, 1991.
```

Figure 2.2. AS/400 Main Menu.

Figure 2.2 is the AS/400 Main Menu you will see when your sign-on is successful. The AS/400 Main Menu groups related system tasks into the listed options in this menu. The more important options that you may frequently use can include:

Option 1. User tasks

The user tasks commands work with user profile, password, library list, job run settings, message handling and spooled files handling, and so forth.

Option 4. Files, libraries, and folders

This option includes those commands that manipulate database and nondatabase files, libraries, and folders.

Option 5. Programming

This option brings up the Programming Development Manager (PDM), which you will need to edit and compile your CL and other HLL programs.

To run any command, you can either choose the command from the command menu or type in the command name at the system command line. The Command Entry panel provides the place for the user to enter the system commands. To activate the Command Entry panel now, you can enter:

```
call qcmd
```

at the system command line. QCMD is a system program that sets up the Command Entry panel and accepts the commands entered. It examines the command syntax and runs it.

```
                            Command Entry
    Previous commands and messages:

       (No previous commands or messages)




                                                      Bottom
    Type command, press Enter.
    ===> _____

    _____

    F3=Exit   F4=Prompt   F9=Retrieve   F10=Include detailed messages
    F11=Display full      F12=Cancel    F13=User support   F16=System main menu
```

Figure 2.3. Command Entry panel.

Figure 2.3 is the Command Entry panel. There are several very important function keys that you should learn to use:

• Retrieve key (<F9>)
• Help key (<HELP>)
• Prompt key (<F4>)

You can use the function key <F9> to retrieve previous commands. There are two ways to retrieve previous commands: you can move the cursor to a previous command and press <F9>, or just press <F9> to retrieve commands one at a time in reverse chronological order.

Another function key that you will need frequently is the online Help key. Simply move the cursor to the spot where you have a problem and press <HELP>. The Help key facility provides helpful information at the field level. If you need even more detailed information, you can press the <F2> Extended Help key for more information.

The Prompt key <F4> is another function key that makes your life easier. If you cannot remember the syntax of the command, simply type in the command name and then press <F4>; the prompt screen appears and helps you to complete entering the parameters.

Tip

If you are not sure which command to use to accomplish your purpose, press <F4> to bring up the Command Menu. The commands are grouped by their functionalities on this menu.

We will not go into the details of the AS/400 security concept here. However, we should be familiar with the security levels of the AS/400. We can find out the security level of our AS/400:

```
DSPSYSVAL SYSVAL(QSECURITY)
```

DSPSYSVAL (Display System Value) is the command to display the system values of the AS/400. The system values are a part of the system internal; they are a set of parameters that control the operation of the machine. Security level is one of these values.

When the security level is set at 10, anyone can sign on to the system using any user profile. No password is required, and the user would have all kinds of object authority on the system.

When the security level is set at 20, a user who wants to get access to the system must sign on with a valid user profile, and a password is required. However, at this security level a user can still have all kinds of object operational and object management authority to the objects on the system.

The recommended security level is 30 since it provides more protection to the objects on the system. When the security level is set at 30, the user profile and password are always required to sign on to the system. At the same time, certain object operational and object management authorities are needed before any action can be performed on the objects. Therefore, we can selectively assign object authorities to authorized users to protect the object from any illegal access.

When the security level is set at 40, any access to the system objects are not allowed unless the user has been explicitly granted the authority to the objects. Therefore, security level 40 provides the highest level of protection.

2.2.2. Learn to Use the PDM

PDM stands for Programming Development Manager. It is not a part of the AS/400 operating system; it is a licensed product, separately priced.

The purpose of PDM is to give the programmer a consistent interface to the development tools. The advantage of using PDM is that it presents lists of items and allows entry of options on the menu to manipulate libraries, objects, and file members.

To start the Programming Development Manager (PDM), type the following command:

```
STRPDM
```

which stands for Start Programming Development Manager at the command line. Figure 2.4 shows you the Main Menu for the Programming Development Manager.

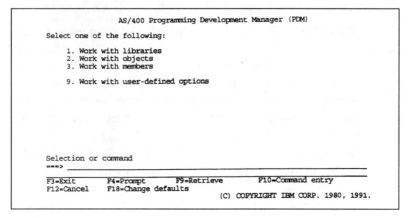

```
                    AS/400 Programming Development Manager (PDM)

        Select one of the following:

              1. Work with libraries
              2. Work with objects
              3. Work with members

              9. Work with user-defined options




        Selection or command
        ===>
        _____
        F3=Exit        F4=Prompt      F9=Retrieve        F10=Command entry
        F12=Cancel     F18=Change defaults
                                              (C) COPYRIGHT IBM CORP. 1980, 1991.
```

Figure 2.4. Programming Development Manager Main Menu.

The STRPDM command presents a menu that shows the choices from which to select. You can work with each type directly with the WRKXXXPDM command, for example, WRKLIBPDM for libraries, WRKOBJPDM for objects, and WRKMBRPDM for file members.

The PDM Main Menu includes the following options:

Option 1. Work with libraries

Use this option to change the library type and the text description of the library, copy objects from one library to another, delete the library, display the list of objects in the library, rename the library, save and restore the library, display the library description, and work with the objects in the library.

Option 2. Work with objects

Any object in a library can be a physical file, a logical view, a compiled program, a message queue or a job queue, and so forth. This option lets you work with the object descriptions, copy the contents of the object to another, delete or rename the object, save or restore the object, move the object to another library, and so forth.

Option 3. Work with members

Any file on the AS/400 can have multiple members. A member is defined as a subset of the data within the file. This option lets you work with the members in a file.

To edit any source program, choose option 3 from the PDM Main Menu and specify the library and the source file names. The list of members in the source file will be displayed as shown in Figure 2.5.

```
                    Work with Members Using PDM

   File . . . . . .   QCLSRC
      Library . . . .    JOE            Position to  . . . . . _____

   Type options, press Enter.
      2=Edit         3=Copy       4=Delete      5=Display    6=Print
      7=Rename       8=Display description      9=Save       13=Change text ...

   Opt  Member      Type      Text
   __   CPYTOTAP    CLP       EXAMPLE OF USING CPYTOTAP COMMAND
   __   RPG002CL    CLP



                                                              Bottom
   Parameters or command
   ===>
   F3=Exit          F4=Prompt              F5=Refresh          F6=Create
   F9=Retrieve      F10=Command entry      F23=More options    F24=More keys
```

Figure 2.5. Work with Members using PDM menu.

Each member within a file is identified by its member name. You cannot have two members with the same name in the same file, even though their types are different.

When you are inside the Work with Members using PDM menu, press function key <F6> to create and add a new member to the source physical file.

Choose a name for your program, determine its program type (CLP for our example), and you will see a blank screen where you can start editing your CL program.

When you are inside the editing screen, PDM would start the SEU (Source Entry Utility) with all of the default settings. The following function keys may be helpful to you later on:

1. <F13> to change the session default
   The session parameters include:
   • full screen or half screen to roll,
   • uppercase input only,
   • source type,
   • whether syntax checking is on
      etc.
   You can set the syntax checking flag to Y; then each line of source code you enter would be checked for syntax error.

14> to find and change a character string
e this option to find any character string and substitute it
th another string.

Tip

Function key <F14> only scans through one member. If you
want to scan through every member in the source file, you can
use the FNDSTRPDM command. You can even run this command outside PDM.

---

3. <F15> to browse and copy another source program
   This option provides a split screen for the display of another
   source member while you are still in editing mode.

Figure 2.6 is a small program that you can enter and test. The
statement identifiers are shown alongside the source codes. They are
not part of the source codes but are provided by the Source Entry
Utility when editing is underway. After you have entered the source
codes, press <F3> to exit and save the member.

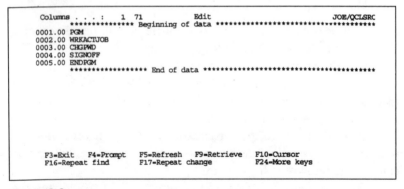

```
 Columns . . . :    1  71          Edit                        JOE/QCLSRC
           *************** Beginning of data ******************************
 0001.00 PGM
 0002.00 WRKACTJOB
 0003.00 CHGPWD
 0004.00 SIGNOFF
 0005.00 ENDPGM
           ***************** End of data ********************************





         F3=Exit    F4=Prompt    F5=Refresh   F9=Retrieve    F10=Cursor
         F16=Repeat find         F17=Repeat change           F24=More keys
```

Figure 2.6.

Tip

If you do not have a source physical file, create one using the
CRTSRCPF (Create Source Physical File) command.

It is a good practice to have separate source files for different source types, for example, QDDSSRC for the data description specifications, QCLSRC for the CL source programs,
and QRPGSRC for the RPG source programs.

After you have saved the member, you can now compile this program by batch or interactively. When you select option 14 (compile) for any source member, PDM would run the appropriate CRTXXXPGM command based on the member type.

On the PDM menu, if you key in an option and press <ENTER>, the associated command is run; if you press <F4> instead, PDM would invoke the command prompter so that you can change some of the parameter values.

Figure 2.7 is a work flow diagram for using the PDM to edit and compile a source program.

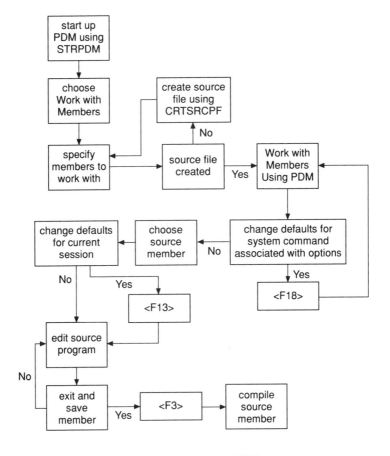

Figure 2.7. Work flow diagram for using the PDM.

decided to compile the program by batch and outside
can submit the compilation to a job queue. A batch job is
an interactive job and is created on the AS/400 by the
Submit Job (SBMJOB) or Batch Job (BCHJOB) commands. Every
batch job submitted lines up in a job queue to wait for its turn to be
run. A batch job can be submitted by an interactive job or from another batch job.

Tips

Use the SBMJOB (Submit Job) command to submit the compilation job by batch.

On the other hand, you can run the CRTCLPGM (Create
CL Program) command at the system command line for interactive compilation.

2.2.3. Learn a Few More Commands

Use the Work with Submitted Jobs (WRKSBMJOB) command to
find out the current status of the batch job that you have submitted:

    WRKSBMJOB

Figure 2.8 shows the display of the Work with Submitted Jobs
command.

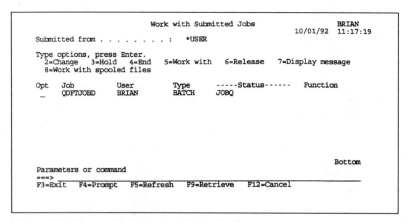

Figure 2.8. Work with Submitted Jobs display.

In the display in Figure 2.8, you can see that the status of the compilation job that you have submitted is JOBQ, which means that it is still in the job queue and waiting to be selected by the system to run.

The possible status of a batch job can be:

1. JOBQ — the job is successfully submitted and is still in the job queue waiting for its turn for execution
2. ACTIVE — the job is running
3. OUTQ — the job was ended and its output has been written to spooled files in an output queue

If the job is submitted successfully to the job queue, the system should return a message to you that indicates the assigned job name and also the job queue the job is waiting at.

Suppose our compilation job is submitted to a job queue named QBATCH in library QGPL; we can check the current status of the job queue using the Work with Job Queue (WRKJOBQ) command:

```
WRKJOBQ QBATCH
```

Figure 2.9, below, shows the current status of the job queue QBATCH.

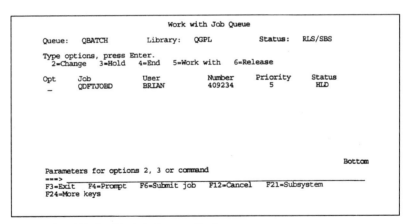

Figure 2.9. Work with Job Queue display.

The WRKJOBQ command displays all the jobs waiting in the named job queue and their current job status as well. When the job status is HLD, the job has been put on hold. When it is RLS, the job is released from the on hold position and ready to run. In Figure 2.9

above we can see that our submitted job is still being put on hold; we should release it and it will be selected by the system to run.

After we release the job from Held status, we can do a Work with Submitted Jobs (WRKSBMJOB) again and this time we would see that the current status of the job is ACTIVE, meaning that this job is now running. We can also tell from the FUNCTION column the command being called by our job. In our example, the command called by our job is CRTCLPGM (Create CL Program), which compiles the CL program.

While the compilation is still underway, we can do a Work with Active Jobs (WRKACTJOB) to display the statistics on the active jobs in the system.

    WRKACTJOB

Figure 2.10 shows the display of the Work with Active Jobs command.

```
                         Work with Active Jobs                    BRIAN
                                                   10/01/92  11:27:37
    CPU %:   55.7      Elapsed time:   00:06:55   Active jobs:    45

    Type options, press Enter.
      2=Change   3=Hold   4=End     5=Work with    6=Release   7=Display message
      8=Work with spooled files   13=Disconnect  ...

    Opt  Subsystem/Job  User      Type  CPU %  Function      Status
      _    BATCH1        QSYS      SBS    .1                  DEQW
      _    BDS           QSYS      SBS    .0                  DEQW
      _      PRT01       QSYSOPR   WTR    .0                  EVTW
      _      SYS36LSR    QSYSOPR   WTR    .2                  ICFW
      _    QPGMR         QSYS      SBS    .0                  DEQW
      _    QBATCH        QSYS      SBS    .0                  DEQW
      _      QDFTJOBD    BRIAN     BCH   5.6    CMD-CRTCLPGM  RUN
      _    QCMN          QSYS      SBS    .0                  DEQW
      _      QDFTJOBD    QUSER     EVK    .0   *  -PASSTHRU   EVTW
                                                                More...
    Parameters or command
    ===>
    F3=Exit      F5=Refresh  F10=Restart statistics   F11=Display elapsed data
    F12=Cancel   F23=More options   F24=More keys
```

Figure 2.10. Work with Active Jobs display.

The figure shows all the jobs running in the system, including batch jobs, interactive jobs, communication jobs, spooling jobs, and so forth. We can see that the job we have submitted is running in a subsystem called QBATCH.

In brief, a subsystem is a logical division of the main memory. It is set up by establishing a set of parameters that control the running environment on the system. From the display, we can see that this compilation job has taken up 5.6 percent of the CPU resources within the elapsed time. We can also see that the job type is BCH (Batch Job) and its status is RUN.

Sometimes you may find that there are too many jobs submitted to the same job queue; then you may want to throw your job to another job queue that is not that busy. However, you must have job control authority (*JOBCTL) as one of your special authorities in your user profile.

The special authorities allow a user to perform system control operations such as:

1. Using system service tools (*SECADM)
2. Controlling user jobs (*JOBCTL)
3. Controlling spooled files (*SPLCTL)
4. Backup and restore (*SAVSYS)
   etc.

Special authority is defined in the user profile.

After the job is completed, the job status becomes OUTQ, as you would see in the WRKSBMJOB display. You can look at the spooled files created by the job and if the job is not successful, you may want to read the job log and the compiled listing to find out what is wrong.

Figure 2.11 shows the work flow diagram for using the different job control commands.

Command Summary

STRPDM	Start the Programming Development Manager
WRKLIBPDM	Work with Libraries using PDM
WRKOBJPDM	Work with Objects using PDM
WRKMBRPDM	Work with Members using PDM
CRTSRCPF	Create Source Physical File
SBMJOB	Submit Job
CRTCLPGM	Create CL Program
WRKSBMJOB	Work with Submitted Jobs
WRKJOBQ	Work with Job Queue
WRKACTJOB	Work with Active Jobs

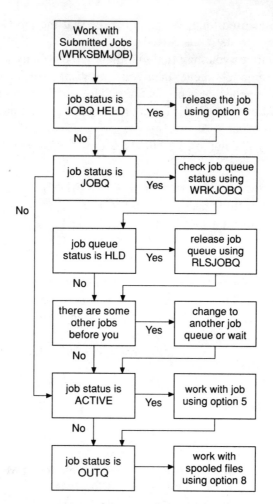

Figure 2.11. Work flow diagram for job control.

Exercises

2.1. Explain the following terms:
Object
Library
Library list
Job
Job descriptions

Interactive job
Batch job
Job queue
Subsystem
Subsystem descriptions

2.2. What is the Command Entry panel? How do you get there?

2.3. What is the Programming Development Manager? How do you get there?

2.4. What is a source member? Briefly describe the procedures of editing a source member.

2.5. Find out the different ways of compiling a source member into an executable object.

2.6. What command would show you the current status of your submitted jobs?

3

The Basic Elements

This chapter is about variables, operators, and expressions used in the control language programs.

Control language (CL) programs provide a vehicle for communication between the user and the machine. When we talk about the machine, we mean the "logical" machine rather than the physical machine. The design of the AS/400 has conceptualized and encapsulated the functions of a physical machine into system object descriptions, and we are working with these object descriptions instead of with the physical machine directly.

A control language (CL) program is actually a sequence of control language commands running by batch. The basic elements of a CL program include the control language command and the program construct that organizes these commands into meaningful structures. If we analyze the control language commands on the AS/400, we can see that the CL commands consist of smaller elements that include the verb, modifier, object, and parameters. On the other hand, the program constructs include the operand and operator arranged in expressions or arguments according to strict semantic rules of the AS/400.

There are over 700 CL commands on the AS/400. Most of these CL commands can be run directly at the system command line interactively or can be invoked from the AS/400 menus, and some of them can be coded into source file and be compiled into a program. Most of the CL commands have the following general syntax:

```
verb-modifier-object parameters(parameter-values)
```

For example, the command that we use to compile and create a physical file is called Create Physical File (CRTPF). Here CREATE is the verb and FILE is the object. However, there are so many types of files on the AS/400 that you need to specify which kind of file you want to create; the modifier PHYSICAL serves that purpose. There are some parameters associated with the command, and some of them have to be specified when you run the command. The compulsory parameters include the compiled object name, but the others are optional, like the maximum size of the file and so on.

Therefore the CRTPF command that you want to run can have the following syntax:

```
CRTPF FILE(library-name/file-name) +
   SRCFILE(library-name/file-name) +
      SRCMBR(member-name)
```

There are two major groups of CL commands. The first group of commands invokes the operating system to perform some actions on objects; most of the commands fall into this category. The second group consists of program constructs commands, for instance, the IF command, the ELSE command, the DO command, the ENDDO command, the PGM command, and the ENDPGM command.

The first group of commands can be subdivided into several subgroups:

- Object management commands
- File commands
- Work management commands
- Print commands
- Spooling commands
- Programming commands
- Database commands
- Message-handling commands

Since the number of commands is large, you may not know every command and its syntax in order to perform the actions you want. The general rule is to think of the verb first followed by the object. For example, if you want to create the object, the first three characters of the command would be CRT, and if the object you want to create is a program, the ending three characters should be PGM. The modifier, as mentioned above, specifies what type of object it is, and if you want to compile a CL program, the modifier would be the two-character descriptor CL. Therefore the CL command that creates a CL program would be CRTCLPGM.

If you want to find out all the commands related to a specific type of object, either press the function key <F4> for the Command Menu, or type

```
GO CMDXXX
```

at the command line, where XXX stands for the object type. For instance, if you want the menu of the commands related to job, type

```
GO CMDJOB
```

at the command line.

Although there are different sets of commands dealing with different object types, the same set of syntax rules apply to all of them:

1. Each command has to follow the order of parameters.
2. Each command requires the keyword in front of a parameter.
3. System parameters require the * before the parameter.

A command operates on an object and the object is the smallest unit of operation on the AS/400 system. This chapter describes how a CL program operates on an object using commands, and we will look into the operations that are employed to manipulate them.

The function of control language programs is to perform certain actions on the specified object in order to achieve some specific purposes. The typical CL program would consist of the following parts:

1. PGM statement
   The PGM statement is optional; it marks the beginning of the program source codes.
2. Declarations (DCL and DCLF statements)
   The DCL statements declare all the program variables that would be used in the program. For every CL program, exactly one Declare File (DCLF) statement is allowed. After the declarations of variables and files, we can construct the program logic using different CL commands.

3.1. Variable Name and Declaration

CL programs are sequences of CL commands coded to run in batch. They can be edited, compiled, and debugged in advance and executed at any time like other HLL programs. Each CL command in the program has to follow the syntax rule. The general syntax and the different components of a CL command are shown in Figure 3.1.

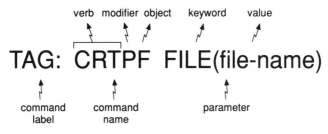

Figure 3.1. Components of a CL command.

The command label is optional; it is used as an identifier for the command statement inside the program. It can be used together with the GOTO command to form a loop, since we do not have any structured programming construct in CL that has the same functionality of a "while" loop or "for" loop.

The command name identifies the specific action you want to perform on the object. As we have mentioned earlier, the command name usually consists of three parts: verb, modifier, and object. The parameters of the command are specified by the keyword and the value for that keyword. Each command has a different number of parameters, and even the same command may have different combinations of parameters in different cases in order to achieve different results.

3.1.1. Functions of the Variables

The primary function of the variables in a CL program is to substitute for the parameter values of the CL command in the program.

Variables are used to contain values for the parameters of the CL command, and the contents of it can be changed from time to time by the instructions in the program. These variables exist in main storage and are only accessible by the program that declared them unless they are passed as parameters to another program. Once a variable is assigned to represent the value for a CL command parameter, the current value of the variable is substituted in the parameter it is assigned to in the command when the command is run. That is, the variable value is passed to the command as if the user had specified it at the system command line.

The variables exist in the main memory and would only last during the lifetime of the program. The location of the variables are identified by name. We should bear in mind that variables are not objects, they are not stored in any library, and they do not exist after the program that created them is removed from the program stack. The variable contains a value that can be changed by the program instructions, depending on the program logic, while the program is still on the program stack of the current job.

3.1.2. Changes in Variable Values

The value contained in a variable can be changed when:

1. the Change Variable (CHGVAR) command is run
   The Change Variable (CHGVAR) command is an assignment operator that assigns a value to a variable. For example, the value of variable &X is changed from its previous value to a constant value of 10 as follows:

   ```
   CHGVAR VAR(&X) VALUE(10)
   ```

   This expression simply means that the value 10 is assigned to the variable &X.

2. the variable is being passed as a parameter
   When a variable is passed as a parameter from the calling program to the called program, its value is subject to change by the instructions in the called program. When the called program is ended and control is passed back to the calling program, the variable passed as a parameter would contain the value last updated by the called program. When the calling program receives that parameter from the called program, the value of the variable is already changed.The calling program would then use that value for subsequent instructions following the program call.

3. the variable receives a value from the data area
   A variable can be assigned a new value by receiving from a data area using the Retrieve Data Area (RTVDTAARA) command.

   ```
   RTVDTAARA DTAARA(data-area-name) RTNVAR(variable-
   name)
   ```

4. the variable receives a value from a display device
   A variable can be assigned a new value by receiving the value from a display device as input by the user.

5. the variable receives a value from a message
   The CL program can send an inquiry or notify message to a message queue and receive the reply and return its values to variables defined in the program. Variables can be assigned new values by receiving a reply from the reply message queue. But these variables must be declared before they can be used in a program.
6. the variable receives a value from a file
   A variable can be assigned a new value when receiving the value from a file. The file need not be a display file; it could be a database file as well.

3.1.3. Declaring Variable

Every variable used in a CL program must be declared. If your program refers to CL variables without first declaring them, you would receive an error message generated in the compilation as follows:

```
CPD0727 40 Variable XXX is referred to but not declared.
```

This message simply indicates that your program has made reference to a variable named XXX but it is not declared before it is used.

Variables used in a CL program must be declared using the Declare (DCL) command. Figure 3.2 shows you the syntax for a DCL command.

DCL VAR(variable-name) TYPE(data-type) LEN(length) VAL(initial-value)

Figure 3.2. Components of the Declare (DCL) command.

The keyword VAR (Variable) in the DCL command is where you specify the variable name. A variable name used in a CL program must not be longer than 11 characters. Figure 3.3 shows the naming rule for CL variables.

The variable name must always be preceded with an ampersand (&). The second character must be alphabetic (A–Z) or any of the special characters #, @, or $. The third to eleventh characters can be alphanumeric (A–Z, 0–9), #, @, $, period(.), or underscore(_).

1	2	3	4	5	6	7	8	9	10	11
&	V	A	R	I	A	B	L	E	0	1

Position 1:   always an ampersand (&)
Position 2:   alphabetic (A–Z), #, @, or $
Positions 3–11: alphanumeric (A–Z, 0–9), #, @, $,
                        period (.), or underscore (_)

Figure 3.3. Naming rule for CL variables.

The keyword TYPE (data type) in the DCL command is where you specify the data type of the variable. The data types allowed in CL programming include:

1. Character
   A character variable can be as long as 9999 bytes in length; if you do not specify the initial value (VALUE) in the DCL command, the compiler would take blank as the default.
2. Decimal
   A decimal variable can be up to 15 digits in length with 9 after the decimal. If you do not specify the initial value (the VALUE parameter in the DCL command), the compiler would take 0 as the default. One thing to bear in mind is that unlike RPG programs, we cannot specify packed or un-packed decimals since all decimals are in packed format in CL programs.
3. Logical
   A logical variable must be either 0 or 1 in value; if you do not specify the initial value, the compiler will take 0 as the default.

The keyword VAL (Initial Value) in the DCL command specifies the initial value of the variable; this parameter is optional. For example,

```
DCL VAR(&A) TYPE(*DEC) VALUE(1234.56)
```

would give an initial value of 1234.56 to variable &A when it is declared.

When the initial value is not specified, the compiler takes the default initial value for the specified data type. The following are some general rules regarding variable declarations using the DCL command.

1. When the keyword LEN (length of variable) is omitted, the compiler takes the length of the initial value as the length of the variable, for example,

   ```
   DCL VAR(&A) TYPE(*DEC) VALUE(1234.56)
   ```

   The declare statement above does not specify the length of the variable &A. In this case, the compiler would take (6 2) as the length of the variable &A because the initial value 1234.56 is 6 digits in length of which 2 are decimals.

2. when both length and initial value are omitted, for example,

   ```
   DCL VAR(&A) TYPE(*DEC)
   ```

   the declare statement specifies only the data type of the variable. If the length of the variable and its initial value are not declared in the DCL command, the compiler takes the default length for the corresponding data type on the AS/400 system.

Type	Default length
Decimal	15,5
Character	32
Logical	1

   The default length for a decimal data type is 15 digits of which 5 digits are decimals. For the character variable type the default is 32 bytes in length and for the logical variable type the default length is 1 byte.

3. The maximum length of the variables is checked by the compiler.

   You will receive the error message "Length specified is too long for variable type" if the length specified in the DCL statement has exceeded the limit for the data type. For example,

   ```
   DCL VAR(&A) TYPE(*DEC) LEN(30 10)
   DCL VAR(&B) TYPE(*CHAR) LEN(100)
   ```

   You will receive error messages when you compile the program that contains these statements.

4. When you define a qualified name in a CL program, you need to define separate variables for different components in the qualified name.

   For example, when you want to run a CL command on a file named FILE1 in the library called LIB01, you can make reference to the file using its qualified name:

   ```
   DCL VAR(&LIB) VALUE(LIB01)
   DCL VAR(&FILE) VALUE(FILE1)
   CL-command parameter(&LIB/&FILE)
   ```

However, you should always declare separate variables for the file name &FILE and the library name &LIB, and you should not declare one variable to contain the whole string of the library name and file name like this:

```
DCL VAR(&NAME) TYPE(*CHAR) LEN(20)
CHGVAR VAR(&NAME) VALUE('LIB01/FILE1')
```

If you declare one variable and assign to this variable the file name and library name with a slash (/) in between, you may not receive any error message when you compile the program, but you certainly will get an operating system-level error message when you call the program.

3.2. Constants

Constants are literals and remain unchanged during the lifetime of the program. There are three types of constants in CL programming.

3.2.1. Character Constants

A character constant is a string of characters in either quoted or unquoted format. Both formats of character string can contain as many as 2000 characters. Some of the character strings must be quoted because they contain some special characters that are invalid when unquoted. These special characters include:

- Blank
- Colon (:)
- Percent (%)
- Question mark (?)
- Semicolon (;)

Therefore, the following character strings are all *invalid* character strings when they are unquoted:

JOHN SMITH (a blank exists in between)
NAME : (a colon is included)
28% (a percent sign is included)
HOW LONG? (a question mark is included)
ONE; TWO (a semicolon is included)

Instead, if you quote the above character strings as shown below they become *valid* character strings:

'JOHN SMITH'
'NAME : '
'28%'
'HOW LONG?'
'ONE; TWO'

On the other hand, some of the other special characters are allowed in unquoted strings; they include:

1. Asterisk (*)

   When an asterisk is used as the first character of a variable name, it indicates a predefined value, for example,

   *LIBL
   *OUTQ

   where *LIBL stands for the predefined value for library list, and *OUTQ stands for the predefined value for output queue. When the asterisk is used at the end of a name, it indicates that the name is a generic name, for example, PGM* includes every name beginning with the three characters PGM.

2. Slash (/)

   A slash is used as a connector in qualified names, for example,

   ```
   TEST/FILE1
   ```

   stands for a file called FILE1 in a library called TEST.

3. +, -, ., and ,

   These special characters are used with decimal constants, for example,

   +12.34,
   -34.56

   In an unquoted string of numeric characters, an optional decimal point (as indicated by a . or ,) and an optional leading sign (+ or -) are valid.

4. Parentheses (and)

   Parentheses (and) are valid when used as the delimiters in keyword values in a CL command or to indicate the order of evaluation in a nested expression.

5. The special characters +, -, *, /, &, |, <, >, and = are valid in themselves.

3.2.2. Decimal Constants

A decimal constant is a numeric string consisting of one or more digits (0–9) and preceded by a sign (+ or -), but the sign is optional. The
decimal constant can have up to a maximum of 15 digits in length in
which no more than 9 digits after the decimal point are allowed.
Therefore, a decimal constant can have up to a maximum of 17 characters in length (15 digits, the decimal point, and the sign). The following are valid decimal constants:

    +123.456
    123.456
    -543.221
    -543,221
    -.098
    +123456.789012345

3.3. Arithmetic Operators

Operators in CL programming are used to indicate the action to be
performed on the operands in the expression, or evaluate the relationship between the operands. The simplest expression in CL programming only contains two operands and an operator. However, it
is very common to combine two or more expressions to form a complex expression.

3.3.1. Types of Expressions

There are four types of expressions in CL programming:

1. Arithmetic expression, e.g.,

   ```
   &X + &Y - &Z (add variable X to Y and subtract Z from the
   sum)
      &SALES / 100 (divide the variable SALES by the con-
   stant 100)
   ```

2. Character string expression, e.g.,

   ```
      John || Smith (concatenate character strings "John"
   with "Smith")
   ```

3. Logical expression, e.g.,

   ```
      &VAR1 & &VAR2 (test if both boolean variables VAR1
   and VAR2 are true)
   ```

```
&HOT | &HUMID (test if boolean variables HOT and HU-
MID are true)
```

4. Relational expression, e.g.,

```
&VAR1 > &VAR2 (test if variable VAR1 is greater than
VAR2)
```

```
&COLOR = 'RED' (test if variable COLOR contains the
value RED)
```

A complex expression contains multiple operands and multiple operators. When the program logic becomes more and more complex, we need to construct complex expressions for arithmetic operations and logical evaluation in our CL programs. The following is an example of a complex expression where several levels of nested expression are employed to evaluate the final value:

```
IF (((&VAR1 + &VAR2) > &CONS1) & ((&NAME1 || &NAME2) <
              &CONS2))
```

However, no matter how complex an expression it is, every kind of expression still has to obey the same rules as a simple expression. The rules that apply universally include:

1. There is only one operator allowed between two operands. The exceptions are:
   - The + or - sign in a signed decimal value, as shown here: `&VAR1 > -1.0` (the variable VAR1 is greater than -1.0) `&X + (-&VAR2)` (the variable X is added to the negative value of VAR2)
   - The negation (*NOT) operator, as shown:
     ```
     &VAR4 & *NOT &VAR5
     &HOT & *NOT &HUMID
     ```

2. A complex expression cannot have more than five nested levels of parentheses. An operator can be specified as a predefined value, that is, you can use *EQ instead of the symbol = in the expression, so the following two expressions are identical:
   ```
   (&X *EQ &Y) & (&Z *EQ &W)
   ```
   is identical to
   ```
   (&X = &Y) & (&Z = &W)
   ```
   The other predefined values are *NE (not equal to), *GT (greater than), *GE (greater than or equal to), *LT (less than), and *LE (less than or equal to).

3. All predefined values must have blanks on both sides when used as an operator in an expression, so the following expression is invalid:

```
(&X*EQ&Y) & (&Z*EQ&W)
```

Instead you should leave at least one blank on both sides of *EQ so that the expression should look like this:

```
(&X *EQ &Y) & (&Z *EQ &W)
```

3.3.2. Types of Operators

There are four arithmetic operators:

1. Addition (+)
2. Subtraction (-)
3. Multiplication (*)
4. Division (/)

The priority of multiplication and division (* and /) are higher than that of addition and subtraction (+ and -). The operands in an arithmetic expression must be defined as decimal constants or decimal variables. The result of an arithmetic expression is always decimal.

Arithmetic operands can be signed or unsigned; however, the sign is optional. Unlike the predefined values, the compiler does not care whether you put blanks around the operator or not, so the following expression is acceptable.

```
CHGVAR VAR(&A) VALUE(&B+&C)
```

However, for the purpose of readability it is better to have spaces around the operators:

```
CHGVAR VAR(&A) VALUE(&B + &C)
```

One exception is the division operator (/), where you must insert at least one blank preceding the division operator. The following expressions are both acceptable:

```
CHGVAR VAR(&A) VALUE(&B / &C)
CHGVAR VAR(&A) VALUE(&B /&C)
```

But the expression involving the following division operator is not acceptable because the compiler would regard &B/&C as a qualified name (like library-name/file-name) rather than as a division expression (variable C divides B).

```
CHGVAR VAR(&A) VALUE(&B/&C)
```

Another thing you need to bear in mind when formulating arithmetic expressions is that the denominator must not be equal to zero; otherwise the operating system would give you an error message at machine level (error message MCH1211) when you run the program.

A complex arithmetic expression may look like this:

```
CHGVAR &A (&B * 0.5 * &CONST1 - 1)
```

The expression would be evaluated according to the order of precedence.

The + or - signs in CL programming can be used as a continuation character when it is placed as the last character in a line, and in that case, it is not counted as an arithmetic operator. See Figure 3.4 for an illustration.

```
          ...+... 1 ...+... 2 ...+... 3 ...+... 4 ...+... 5 ...+... 6 ...+... 7
          ******* Beginning of data **************************************
0001.00 PGM
0001.03              DCL     VAR(&A) TYPE(*DEC) LEN(5 0)
0001.04              DCL     VAR(&B) TYPE(*DEC) LEN(5 0)
0001.05              DCL     VAR(&C) TYPE(*DEC) LEN(5 0)
0001.06              CHGVAR  VAR(&A) VALUE(&B / &C) /* this is a test of +
0001.07                      the plus sign used as a continuation +
0001.08                      character in a control language program +
0001.09                      instead of an arithmetic operator and +
0001.10                      this is a comment line for this change +
0001.11                      variable command */
0005.00 ENDPGM
          ***************** End of data *****************************************
```

Figure 3.4. Using + sign as continuation character.

3.4. Relational and Logical Operators and Operand Types

3.4.1. Relational and Logical Operators

The relational and logical operators, when applied to the operands, evaluate the logical value (which is a boolean value of true or false) of a logical expression or statement. In CL programming, the relational operators include the following:

Symbol	Predefined value	Meaning
=	*EQ	equal
>	*GT	greater than
<	*LT	less than

(continued)

Symbol	Predefined value	Meaning
>=	*GE	greater than or equal
<=	*LE	less than or equal
¬=	*NE	not equal
¬>	*NG	not greater than
¬<	*NL	not less than

3.4.2. Types of Operands Allowed in Relational Expression

The operands in a relational expression can be:

1. Arithmetic operands
   For example, in the following IF statement, (&A + &B) is an arithmetic expression that is used as one of the operands in the relational expression that involves the > sign.

   ```
   IF COND((&A + &B) > &C)
   THEN (CHGVAR VAR(&RESULT) VALUE(&A + &B))
   ```

2. Character string operands
   In the following IF statement, &A is defined as a character string and is used as one of the operands in the relational expression that involves the comparison of two character strings.

   ```
   IF COND(&A = 'texas')
   THEN (CHGVAR VAR(&RESULT) VALUE(&A))
   ```

3. Logical variables or constants
   In the following IF statement, variable &A is defined as a logical variable that is used as an operand in the relational expression.

   ```
   IF COND(&A = '1')
   THEN (CHGVAR VAR(&RESULT) VALUE('texas'))
   ```

One very important rule is that only two operands are allowed in each simple relational expression. We must also bear in mind that the data types for both operands in the relational expression must be of the same type. The result of the evaluation of a relational expression is always either TRUE ('1') or FALSE('0').

If the relational expression involves character string variables of different lengths, the shorter one could be expanded internally, with trailing blanks before the relational expression is evaluated. An example is shown in the following statements:

```
DCL VAR(&A) TYPE(*CHAR) LEN(5) VALUE('texas')
DCL VAR(&B) TYPE(*CHAR) LEN(10) VALUE('texas ')
IF COND(&A = &B)
THEN (action-1)
ELSE (action-2)
```

If we incorporate these statements into our CL program, we would see that the program would evaluate the two character strings as identical, and it would take action-1 as the result.

To evaluate a relational expression, the rule is:

1. Character variables are compared according to the EBCDIC collating sequence.
2. Arithmetic variables are compared arithmetically.
3. Logical variables are compared arithmetically (i.e., $1 > 0$).

3.4.3. Types of Logical Operators

Logical operators include the following:

Symbol	Predefined value	Meaning
&	*AND	and
|	*OR	or
¬	*NOT	negation

3.4.4. Types of Operands Allowed in Logical Expression

The operands in a logical expression can be:

1. Relational expression
   For instance, in the following IF statement, both expressions
   ```
   &A = &B
   &C > 150
   ```
   are relational expressions used as operands in the logical expression.
   ```
   IF COND((&A = &B) *AND (&C > 150))
   THEN (actions...)
   ```

2. Logical variables or constants
   In the IF statement below, variable &C is defined as a logical variable and it is used as an operand in the logical expression:

   ```
   IF COND((&A = &B) *AND (&C = '1'))
   THEN (actions.....)
   ```

   You can combine two or more logical expressions to form a complex logical expression, but it cannot exceed more than five nested levels of parentheses. The result of the evaluation of a logical expression is always a TRUE ('1') or FALSE ('0'). The *AND operator in the logical expression indicates that all of the operands must return the true value at the same time to give an overall true condition. That is to say, the result of the logical expression is true only when all operands are evaluated as true. The following is the logical value table for the *AND operator:

   ```
   *AND 0 1
   0 0 0
   1 0 1
   ```

   The *OR operator in the logical expression indicates that the result of the logical expression would become true when only one of the operands is evaluated as true.

   ```
   *OR 0 1
   0 0 1
   1 1 1
   ```

   The *NOT operator negates the logical value of the operand. It has a higher priority than the *AND and *OR operators. Therefore it will be evaluated before the logical relationship between the operands is evaluated.

3.5. Assignment Operators

3.5.1. Types of Assignment Operators

There is no assignment operator in control language; remember that the = sign is instead a relational operator in CL programming. Therefore, if we want to assign a new value to a variable, we need to use the CL command Change Variable (CHGVAR).

The following shows the different assignment operators in different programming languages:

var1 = 10 (in C)
var1 := 10 (in Pascal)
MOVE 10 TO VAR1 (in COBOL)
Z-ADD10 VAR1 (in RPG)
CHGVAR VAR1 VALUE(10) (in CL)

Like it or not, CL has the most lengthy expression in assigning value to variable.

The syntax of Change Variable (CHGVAR) is as follows:

```
CHGVAR VAR(variable-name) VALUE(value-expression)
```

The value expression can be a single variable, a constant, or an expression. If the value is an expression, the expression will be evaluated first before it is assigned to the variable. If the variable is a logical variable, the value assigned to it can only be either '1' or '0'. If the variable is a character variable, the value assigned to it can be character or decimal.

3.5.2. Assigning Character to Character

If you assign character value to a character variable, the following rules apply:

1. If the length of the variable is less than the length of the value, the value will be left-justified and truncated.
2. If the length of the variable is greater than the length of the value, the variable will be extended with trailing blanks.

3.5.3. Assigning Decimal to Character

If you assign decimal value to a character variable:

1. The decimal value will be right-justified and padded with leading zeros when it is assigned to the character variable. For example, if the decimal value is 25 and we assign this value to a variable defined as a character variable of length 10, the character variable would become '0000000025'.
2. The character variable must be defined with a length long enough to contain the decimal point and the minus sign (-),

if present, of the decimal value. For example, if the decimal value is -32.5 we can assign this value to a variable defined as a character variable of length 5 or more, but not less. The value of the character variable would become '-32.5' if we define the character variable to be of length 5 exactly.

If you define the length of the character variable to be less than 5, the operating system checks this out and returns with an error message saying that the variable or substring of the variable is too small to hold the result. If you define the length of the character variable to be greater than 5, then the resulting variable is padded with zeros between the sign and the first digit, that is, variable &A would become '-0000032.5' if you define the variable to be of length 10.

If the variable is a decimal variable, the value assigned to it can be character or decimal.

3.5.4. Assigning Decimal to Decimal

If you assign decimal value to a decimal variable:

1. The + or - sign would be placed preceding the leftmost digit. For example, if we assign the decimal value of -123.4 to another decimal variable of length (7,1), that is, seven digits with one digit after the decimal, the decimal variable would become this after we assign the value to it:

    ` -123.4`

2. Truncation would occur if the length of the variable is shorter than the value, for example,

    ```
    DCL VAR(&A) TYPE(*DEC) LEN(7 4)
    DCL VAR(&B) TYPE(*DEC) LEN(7 1)
    CHGVAR VAR(&A) VALUE(123.456)
    CHGVAR VAR(&B) VALUE(&A)
    ```

    The variable &A has value 123.4560 but after it was assigned to the variable &B, which is of a length shorter than &A, its value has become 123.4.

3.5.5. Assigning Character to Decimal

If you assign character value to a decimal variable:

1. The character value must not contain any nondigit.

2. The character value should contain a decimal point. However, the compiler would determine where to place the decimal point if none was found in the character value, and the decimal point would be placed at the rightmost position.

   For example, if we assign a character string '-123.5' to a decimal variable of length (6 1), the resulting decimal variable would become ' -123.5'. If the character value has a + or - sign it will be assigned to the decimal variable. If there is no sign then the compiler would assume that it is positive (+).

3. If the character value contains blanks after the decimal point, the blanks would be eliminated when assigned to the decimal variable.

   For example, if we assign character string '123.5 ' to a decimal variable of length (6,1), the resulting decimal variable would be ' 123.5'.

3.6. String Operators

The operands in a character string expression can be:

1. Character strings (quoted or unquoted)
   For example,
   ```
   John *CAT Smith
   'Happy' *CAT 'Birthday!'
   ```
2. Character variables
   For example,
   ```
   &FIRST *CAT &LAST
   &ADDR1 *CAT &ADDR2
   ```
3. Substring function (%SST or %SUBSTRING)
   For example,
   ```
   %SST(&VAR1 10 5) *CAT %SST(&VAR2 5 6)
   ```
   The result of a character string expression is always a character string.

3.6.1. Types of String Operators

There are three string operators and one substring function that we can use:

1. Concatenation operator (*CAT or ||)

The *CAT operator would just join two character strings as they are and create a result that includes all characters in both strings, including leading blanks, trailing blanks, and embedded blanks. As we have seen from the above example, John *CAT Smith would give John Smith, and 'Happy' *CAT 'Birthday!' would give 'Happy Birthday!'. Blanks would be included in the concatenation. For instance, 'John' *CAT ' Smith' would give 'John Smith'.

2. Blank concatenation operator (*BCAT or |>)

The *BCAT operator would strip out the trailing blanks of the first string and then insert one blank space between the first and second strings. If there are leading blanks in the second string, they would be included as well. If there are trailing blanks in the first character string, they would be eliminated. For example, 'Accounting' *BCAT 'Department' would give 'Accounting Department'. 'John' *BCAT 'Smith' would give 'John Smith'.

3. Trailing concatenation operator (*TCAT or |<)

The *TCAT operator would first strip out the trailing blanks of the first string, then join that with the second string. The second string would not be touched. However, any leading blanks in the second string would be retained in the resulting string. For example,

'12345' *TCAT '67890' gives '1234567890'
'John ' *TCAT 'Smith' gives 'JohnSmith'
'John' *TCAT ' Smith' gives 'John Smith'

3.6.2. System-supplied String Function

The substring function (%SST) can extract a portion of a character string from a local data area and return the extracted value to a defined character variable. The syntax of this function is:

```
%SST(character-string starting-position length)
```

The resulting substring begins at the starting position in the character string as specified in the command above and continues for length as specified.

In the %SST command statement, both the starting position and the length can be CL variables; the restriction is that both of them cannot be zero or negative. This is a built-in function on the AS/400 and it returns a character string that is a subset of another character string. This function can only be coded in the CL program and cannot be run at the command line interactively. This function is used most often in a CHGVAR command or in the IF statement. In a CHGVAR command it can be specified in the variable parameter or in the value parameter.

For example, the substring function is specified in the variable parameter shown here:

```
CHGVAR %SST(&VAR1 1 5) VALUE(ABCDE)
```

Then it will change the first five characters in the character variable &VAR1 to 'ABCDE'. On the other hand, it can be specified in the value parameter:

```
CHGVAR &A %SST(&B 1 3)
```

Then it will extract the first three characters in character string &B and assign its value to another character string &A.

The substring function can be used to simulate an array in a CL program. As CL programs do not support arrays, we can simulate an array by defining a long character string, and we can update and retrieve data from and to the string using the substring function as if this character string were an array.

3.7. Precedence and Order of Evaluation

We will encounter complex expressions that contain multiple operators and multiple operands from time to time. In these cases, the expression is evaluated in a specified order as determined by the individual machine. The only way to alter the determined order and priority is with the use of parentheses. The following table lists the priority and order of evaluation for the operators on the AS/400:

Priority	Operators
1	sign of a decimal value, *NOT (highest priority)
2	*, /
3	+, -
4	*CAT, *BCAT, *TCAT
5	*EQ, *GT, *LT, *GE, *LE, *NG, *NL
6	*AND
7	*OR (lowest priority)

Therefore, in any expression the sign (+ or -) of a decimal value is evaluated first and the logical relationship *OR evaluated last. When an expression contains multiple operators of different priorities, the operations are performed according to the priorities as determined in the above table. However, if the operators in an expression are of the same priority, the operations are performed from left to right in the expression. If parentheses are used, the rule is that the innermost parentheses are evaluated first and the outermost parentheses last.

Command Summary

GO	Go to a menu
DCL	Declare variable in a CL program
DCLF	Declare File in a CL program
CHGVAR	Change the value of a Variable

Exercises

3.1. What are the components in the Declare Variable (DCL) statement?

3.2. What are the variable types acceptable to the CL program?

3.3. Explain the difference between the following expressions:
```
&VAR1/&VAR2
&VAR1 / &VAR2
```

3.4. Explain the difference among the three string operators: *CAT, *TCAT, and *BCAT.

Control Flow

This chapter introduces the control flow constructs in the control language (CL) program.

The function of control language is to perform certain actions on the specified object in order to achieve some specific purpose, for example, create a user profile, submit a batch job, copy a database file, connect a display device to the host computer, power down the system, and so forth. When we write the CL program, we have to consider all the possible situations that may arise or any unexpected events that might happen.

The purpose of the control flow constructs in control language is to specify the particular situations that the program might encounter and the subsequent actions it would take in those situations. The program must evaluate the situation and make a decision. The system would make a predefined determination according to the program logic in the control flow statements.

Figure 4.1 illustrates the different parts of a control language program.

The PGM statement is optional and marks the beginning of the program source codes.

The DCL statements declare all the program variables that are used in the program. For every CL program, exactly one Declare File (DCLF) statement is allowed. After the declarations of variables and file, we can construct the program logic using different CL commands, and this chapter will discuss how to construct these logical arguments systematically and structurally.

```
PGM  PARM(list-of-parameters)
     ·
     ·
     ·
DCL  VAR(variable-name) TYPE(data-type)
     ·
     ·
     ·
DCLF  FILE(file-name)
MONMSG  MSGID(message-identifier)
     ·
     ·
     ·
  Program Logic
     ·
     ·
     ·
ENDPGM
```

Figure 4.1. Parts of a CL program.

In CL programming, there are two types of control flow statements:

1. Conditional
2. Unconditional

We will look into each of these in the following sections.

4.1. Conditional Control Flow

The control language commands coded in a CL program are always processed in a sequential order — from the top to the bottom. Each command in the program will be executed one after the other in the sequence they appear in the program. Control language command programs are not structured programming; they are not intended to be, since control language programs are not designed to manipulate data and perform database tasks that are supposed to be handled by other HLL like RPG, COBOL, and C. Control Language programs are mainly for system tasks. Therefore, there are no program constructs in CL programs corresponding to very common constructs in other HLL. For example, the C language has the FOR loop:

```
for (expression)
{
   action 1;
   action 2;
     ·
     ·
}
```

and the WHILE loop:

```
while (expression)
{
   action 1;
   action 2;
      .
      .
      .
}
```

In RPG, we have the DO WHILE, DO UNTIL, and DO loops:

```
DO WHILE (expression)
   action 1
   action 2
      .
      .
      .

END DO
```

However, in CL programs these structured programming constructs do not exist, and we need to code the loop construct using the combinations of some CL commands in order to achieve the same effects. On the other hand, the sequential order of the commands in a CL program can be altered by using control flow commands simulated as a loop. These commands, when combined, can be used to manipulate the program flow.

There are two kinds of control flow commands: conditional and unconditional.

Conditional branching means that under a certain situation the program may branch to another part of the program for execution rather than follow the sequential order of the commands. But branching would occur if and only if the required situation is satisfied. The IF command is a conditional branching command, since the branching occurs if and only if the logical expression in the IF statement is evaluated as true. When combined with the DO and ELSE commands, we can construct an IF-DO-ELSE statement block that lets the program determine which actions to take under certain conditions.

The syntax of a simple IF statement is:

```
IF COND(logical-expression) THEN(CL-command)
```

The IF statement states that if the logical expression in the COND parameter is evaluated as true, then the CL command as stated in the THEN parameter will be executed, otherwise it will not be. The COND parameter is the decision-making process and the

THEN parameter is the action to be taken after the decision-making process is done.

The COND parameter must contain a logical expression that can be evaluated as true or false.

The COND parameter may contain a complex logical and relational expression, and the evaluation of the expression follows the precedence rules as we have already mentioned in Chapter 3.

The THEN parameter must contain a valid CL command. Once the expression is evaluated as true, the CL command contained in the THEN parameter is processed. Otherwise, the next sequential command following the IF statement would be processed.

Figure 4.2 below is a program that contains some IF statement constructs.

```
                PGM
                DCL        VAR(&COPIES) TYPE(*CHAR) LEN(2)
                DCL        VAR(&JOBD) TYPE(*CHAR) LEN(10)
                DCLF       FILE(MENU) RCDFMT(*ALL)

                CHGVAR     VAR(&COPIES) VALUE('01')
REDSPLY:        SNDRCVF    RCDFMT(FORMAT01)
                IF         (&IN07 *EQ '1') THEN(GOTO CMDLBL(ENDCLPGM))
                IF         COND(&IN06 *NE '1') THEN(GOTO CMDLBL(REDSPLY))

                CHGVAR     VAR(&COPIES) VALUE('03')
INFORM:         SNDRCVF    RCDFMT(FORMAT02)
                IF         COND(&IN06 *NE '1') THEN(GOTO CMDLBL(INFORM))

ENDCLPGM:
                DLTOVR     FILE(*ALL)
                ENDPGM
```

Figure 4.2.

In the program in Figure 4.2, there are three IF statements that have independent tasks to perform. The first IF statement states that if the indicator &IN07 is on, then the program should branch to the statement with label ENDCLPGM, and if the indicator &IN07 is off, then the next IF statement would be processed. The second IF statement states that if the indicator &IN06 is off, then the program would branch to command SNDRCVF, which has label REDSPLY.

The program flow chart for the program in Figure 4.2 is shown in Figure 4.3.

The DO command lets you process a group of CL commands sequentially if the logical expression in the COND parameter is evaluated as true. If the logical expression is true, the CL commands between the DO command and the ENDDO command are processed consecutively. The program in Figure 4.4 has several IF-DO constructs.

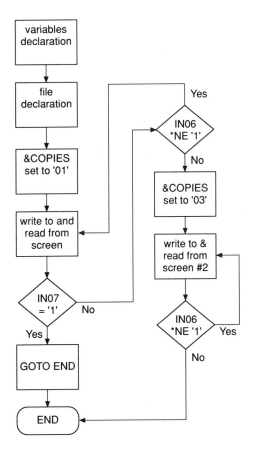

Figure 4.3. Program flow chart.

There are two IF-DO constructs in the program in Figure 4.4. The first one states that if variable &COMPANY is less than or equal to 00 then three CL commands would be executed consecutively. they are:

```
CHGVAR VAR(&IN25) VALUE('1')
CHGVAR VAR(&IN02) VALUE('1')
GOTO CMDLBL(RCDFMT1)
```

Therefore, the basic construct of an IF-DO block is as follows:

```
IF (logical-expression) THEN(DO)
   action 1
   action 2
   .
   .
   .
ENDDO
```

```
                 PGM
                 DCL       VAR(&JOBD) TYPE(*CHAR) LEN(10)
                 DCL       VAR(&COMPANY) TYPE(*CHAR) LEN(2)
                 DCL       VAR(&CPY) TYPE(*CHAR) LEN(2)
RCDFMT1:         SNDRCVF   RCDFMT(FORMAT01)
                 IF        COND(&IN07 *EQ '1') THEN(GOTO CMDLBL(ENDCLPGM))
                           CHGVAR VAR(&IN02) VALUE('0')
                           CHGVAR VAR(&IN25) VALUE('0')
                           CHGVAR VAR(&IN26) VALUE('0')
                 IF        COND(&COMPANY *LE 00) THEN(DO)
                           CHGVAR VAR(&IN25) VALUE('1')
                           CHGVAR VAR(&IN02) VALUE('1')
                           GOTO CMDLBL(RCDFMT1)
                           ENDDO
                 IF        COND(&CPY *LE 00) THEN(DO)
                           CHGVAR VAR(&IN26) VALUE('1')
                           CHGVAR VAR(&IN02) VALUE('1')
                           GOTO CMDLBL(RCDFMT1)
                           ENDDO
LABEL2:          CHGVAR    VAR(&COMPANY)   VALUE('01')
                 CHGVAR    VAR(&CPY) VALUE(2)
                 SBMJOB    RQSDTA('call PGM01') +
                             JOBD(&JOBD) PARM(&CPY &COMPANY)
LABEL3:          SNDRCVF   RCDFMT(FORMAT02)
                 IF        COND(&IN06 *NE '1') THEN(GOTO CMDLBL(LABEL3))
ENDCLPGM:        DLTOVR    *ALL
                 RETURN
                 ENDPGM
```

Figure 4.4. Program with IF-DO constructs.

You can also nest DO commands and IF statements within the DO command; the maximum number of nested IF-DO statements allowed is 10. Figure 4.5 illustrates a nested DO command construct.

```
IF (logical-expression) THEN(DO)
   IF (logical-expression) THEN(DO)
         action 1
         IF (logical-expression) THEN(DO)
               action 1
               action 2
               .
               .
         ENDDO
   ENDDO
   IF (logical-expression) THEN(DO)
         action 1
         action 2
         .
         .
   ENDDO
ENDDO
```

Figure 4.5. Nested DO commands.

The ELSE command indicates the alternative actions to be taken if the logical expression is evaluated as false.

The basic construct of the ELSE command is as follows:

```
IF (logical-expression) THEN(CL-command)
ELSE (CL-command)
```

IF commands can be embedded in the ELSE command, and the construct will look like this:

```
IF (logical-expression) THEN(CL-command)
ELSE CMD(IF (logical-expression) THEN(CL-command))
```

Several CL commands can be grouped and embedded in the ELSE command using the DO command, and the construct would look like this:

```
IF (logical-expression) THEN(CL-command)
ELSE CMD(DO)
   action 1
   action 2
     .
     .
     .
ENDDO
```

The program in Figure 4.6 has two IF-DO-ELSE-DO constructs. The construct is actually very simple:

```
IF (logical-expression) THEN(DO)
   actions
ENDDO
ELSE CMD(DO)
   actions
ENDDO
```

You can always exit from an IF-DO statement block by using a GOTO command. In the program in Figure 4.7 you may see that the program exits from the IF-DO block with a GOTO command.

When the program has executed a GOTO statement, it jumps to the command label and does not return to the original GOTO statement. The RETURN command has the same functionality: it will terminate the current program by removing itself from the program stack, thus any commands coming after the RETURN command will not be executed.

```
             PGM
             DCL          VAR(&WRKSTN) TYPE(*CHAR)  LEN(10)
             DCL          VAR(&EXC) TYPE(*DEC) LEN(6 0)
             DCL          VAR(&COPIES) TYPE(*DEC)   LEN(2 0)
             DCL          VAR(&MOD01)  TYPE(*CHAR)  LEN(23)
             DCL          VAR(&MOD02)  TYPE(*CHAR)  LEN(23)
             DCL          VAR(&MOD03)  TYPE(*CHAR)  LEN(23)
             DCL          VAR(&MOD04)  TYPE(*CHAR)  LEN(23)

             RTVDTAARA    DTAARA(*LDA (1 10)) RTNVAR(&WRKSTN)
             RTVDTAARA    DTAARA(*LDA (20 2)) RTNVAR(&COPIES)

             CHGVAR       VAR(&EXC) VALUE('Y')

           ┌ IF           COND(&EXC *EQ ' ') THEN(DO)
           │ CHGVAR       VAR(&MOD01) VALUE(001 *CAT ' ')
           │ CHGVAR       VAR(&MOD02) VALUE(002 *CAT '99')
           └ ENDDO
           ┌ ELSE         CMD(DO)
           │ CHGVAR       VAR(&MOD01) VALUE(001 *CAT ' ')
           │ CHGVAR       VAR(&MOD02) VALUE(002 *CAT ' ')
           └ ENDDO

           ┌ IF           COND(&EXC *EQ 0) THEN(DO)
           │ CHGVAR       VAR(&MOD03) VALUE(003 *CAT '222222')
           │ CHGVAR       VAR(&MOD04) VALUE(004 *CAT '444444')
           └ ENDDO
           ┌ ELSE         CMD(DO)
           │ CHGVAR       VAR(&MOD03) VALUE(003 *CAT &EXC)
           │ CHGVAR       VAR(&MOD04) VALUE(004 *CAT &EXC)
           └ ENDDO

             CALL         PGM(PGM401) PARM(&MOD01 &MOD02 &MOD03 &MOD04)
ENDCLPGM:    ENDPGM
```

Figure 4.6.

```
FMT **   ...+... 1 ...+... 2 ...+... 3 ...+... 4 ...+... 5 ...+... 6 ...+... 7
         *************** Beginning of data ****************************************
0001.00 PGM
0001.03          DCL      VAR(&A) TYPE(*DEC) LEN(10 2) VALUE(100)
0001.06          DCL      VAR(&B) TYPE(*DEC) LEN(5 0) VALUE(200)
0001.07          DCL      VAR(&RESULT) TYPE(*DEC) LEN(15 5)
0001.08          IF       COND((&A + &B) > 0) THEN(DO)
0001.09          SNDPGMMSG MSG('program is branched to the end and no +
0001.10                       multiplication done')
0001.11          GOTO     CMDLBL(END)
0001.12          ENDDO
0001.13          CHGVAR   VAR(&RESULT) VALUE(&A * &B)
0001.14          SNDPGMMSG MSG('multiplication done')
0005.00  END:    ENDPGM
         ***************** End of data ****************************************
```

Figure 4.7.

4.2. Unconditional Control Flow

Unconditional branching means the program may branch to any command or group of commands located anywhere in the program without evaluation of any condition. The GOTO command achieves this purpose since the execution of the GOTO command does not depend on the evaluation of any logical expression. The CL commands execute sequentially after the unconditional branch, and it does not return to the GOTO statement.

The GOTO statement has the following syntax:

```
GOTO CMDLBL(label)
```

The command label name cannot have more than 10 characters. One thing to bear in mind is that no program cannot have two labels having the same name.

Tip

The GOTO statement would jump to the statement with the command label and does not return.

The program can branch forward or backward by using the GOTO command. As mentioned above, control language is not a structured programming language and we do not have structured constructs like the for loop, the while loop, and the case statement. But we can simulate a loop in a CL program by branching backward.

For example, we have the following program logic:

```
while ( counter is less than 100 )
   action 1
   action 2
   action 3
   increase counter by 1
end of while loop
```

To simulate such a while loop we can do the following in a CL program:

```
LABEL : action 1
        action 2
        action 3
        CHGVAR VAR(counter) VALUE(counter + 1)
        IF (counter is less than 100) THEN(GOTO LABEL)
```

This construct would have the same effect as the while loop above.

Tip

You can simulate a while loop by using the GOTO statement and a command label.

4.3. CALL, Transfer Control, and RETURN

The CALL command in the CL program starts the execution of another program, and it puts the called program on the program stack of the current job.

When you sign on to the AS/400, the system starts an initial program, and the name of this program is placed at level 1 of the program stack. When the initial program calls another program, the called program name is placed at level 2 of the program stack. When the called program ends, its name is removed from the program stack.

The illustration of the program stack and the calling sequence of the programs is shown in Figure 4.8.

Control Sequence	Program Stack
call PGMA	PGMA
PGMA calls PGMB	PGMB PGMA
PGMB calls PGMC	PGMC PGMB PGMA
PGMC ended and returns control to PGMB	PGMB PGMA
PGMB ended and returns control to PGMA	PGMA
PGMA ended	

Figure 4.8. The program stack and the CALL command.

When program A is called, it will be placed at the bottom of the program stack as shown. When program B is called by program A, program B is placed on the stack on top of program A. When program C is called by program B, program C is placed on top of program B on the stack as well. When program C is ended, control is passed back to the program that is immediately below the terminating program on the stack, in this case, program B. Program C would be removed from the stack as well. When program B is ended, it is removed from the program stack and control is returned to the program that lies immediately below it on the stack, namely, program A. The syntax of the CALL command is:

```
CALL PGM(libray/program) PARM(parameter-list)
```

When the called program is ended by the RETURN command or an ENDPGM statement, the called program is removed from the program stack, and control is returned to the program that lies immediately below it on the program stack. Then the CL command after the CALL command in the calling program would be executed.

A CL program can call itself.

The RETURN command removes itself from the program stack. The RETURN command can appear anywhere in the program. The TFRCTL command passes control to the called program and, after control is passed successfully, it removes itself from the program stack. Therefore, when the called program is ended, it passes control back to whatever program lies below it on the program stack instead of the one that has the TFRCTL command coded in it. See Figure 4.9.

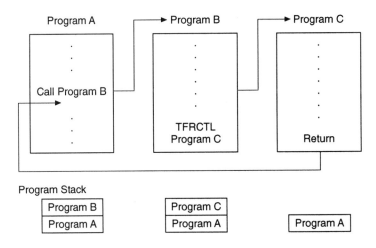

Figure 4.9. Program stack for the Transfer Control command.

Command Summary

GOTO	Jump to a command label
CALL	Call a program
TFRCTL	Transfer Control to another program
RETURN	Return to the calling program from the called program

Exercises

4.1. What are the main parts of a CL program?

4.2. What is the difference between conditional and unconditional control flow?

4.3. Identify which of the following are conditional constructs and which are unconditional:

```
IF;
THEN;
ELSE;
GOTO
```

4.4. What is a program stack? Explain how the following functions affect the program stack:

```
CALL;
TFRCTL;
RETURN
```

5

Library and Object

This chapter introduces you to the world of object and library. Object is the most basic unit on which actions can be performed by the system. Library is the way of organizing objects on the AS/400. Therefore, it is very important to understand these concepts before any CL commands are taught. We will look at the AS/400 concept of object and library, and then the various commands that manipulate them.

5.1. Library and Library List

5.1.1. Organizing Objects on the AS/400

The object is the most basic unit upon which a command performs action on the AS/400. On the AS/400 system, an object is referenced by the object name and object type rather than by its location. You only need to supply the qualified name of the object and the command you want to execute to perform certain operations on the object. You do not really need to know the storage address of the object since it is an internal attribute.

On the AS/400, there are two kinds of object organization methods:

1. By folder
2. By library

A folder is a named object that is used as a directory for documents and other folders. Since folders can be filed within another folder, they are similar to the file system in DOS and UNIX. The folders share a top folder at the top of the hierarchy, just like the root directory, from where the children folders are mounted to the top folder like the branches of a tree. You can create folders and place them within a folder. Data files and programs can be placed in these folders just as files are stored in a subdirectory; see Figure 5.1. This structure was chosen for folders so that PC users can share files within the network; most of the time folders are used in PC support.

AS/400

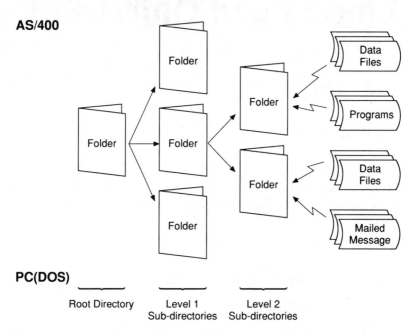

PC(DOS)

Root Directory Level 1   Level 2
      Sub-directories Sub-directories

Figure 5.1. Folders.

Tip

Folders are mostly used for PC support in a network so that users on the PC can share the files on the AS/400.

On the contrary, library is a nonhierarchical organization method on the AS/400 system. Each library itself is an object. However, each library is independent of each other and there are no hierarchies among them, so to speak; all the libraries are placed on the same horizontal level.

The AS/400 has the single-level addressability design, so we cannot mount a library onto another on the disk, and we cannot create a library to be placed within another one. The arrangement of the library system on the AS/400 is nonhierarchical in nature. Figure 5.2 compares the hierarchical file system structure with the nonhierarchical library organization on the AS/400.

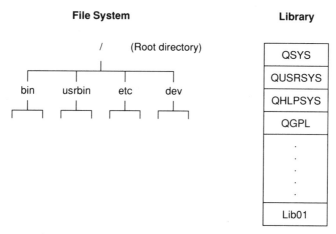

Figure 5.2. Comparison of file system and library organization.

Tip

You may find that each library is stored within the system library QSYS. However, they are not really being stored within QSYS; this is just the referencing method on the AS/400.

5.1.2. Objects Grouped by Library

A library is simply a directory to a group of objects. As mentioned above, the library organization is nonhierarchical and the libraries are addressed independently of each other. There are many ways to group objects into library:

1. Grouped by users
   Objects are grouped into library by their ownership. This method of organization of objects helps you maintain your own objects easily. For example, executable objects (e.g., programs) and database file objects owned by user A can be

grouped into library USERA instead of placing the objects in different libraries and leaving them scattered around on the system. This kind of arrangement makes the maintenance job for the individual a whole lot easier.

2. Grouped by applications

Objects are grouped into library by their application. For example, the accounting database files can be grouped into one library and the payroll database files can be placed into another library. All the programs for the accounting module can be grouped into a library and the payroll programs can be grouped into another library, and so on.

The advantage of this is that this is a very efficient way of arranging the libraries and objects. For example, the accounting data and program libraries are not needed when you run the payroll application. Theoretically speaking, the system performance is better since the library list is shorter now.

The separation of data and programs into libraries also makes it easier for backup and restore purposes, since the database files need daily backup but the programs do not need backup nearly that often. You can even further separate the database files into a number of libraries: master file library, transaction file library, history file library, and so forth. You may need daily backup of the transaction files and history files, but the master files are more static and do not need backup so frequently.

5.1.3. Types of Libraries

There are two types of libraries on the AS/400:

1. Production library
2. Test library

The major difference between a production and a test library is that you can update any files in a test library when you run your program in debug mode, but it would not update any files in a production library when running in debug mode. This would help you protect real data from being updated when you are simply testing your program.

Both production and test libraries are *permanent* libraries; on the other hand, there is a kind of *temporary* library called QTEMP associated with each active job on the system.

Each active job on the system has a working library associated with it; this library is called QTEMP. Each QTEMP is created by the system. However, the QTEMP library created for one job is not the same as one created for another job, although the names are the same. QTEMP is destroyed when the job is ended and any objects stored in it are lost as well.

Sometimes we might want to create temporary objects at runtime for the application; we could choose to place them in QTEMP. Since these temporary objects would be destroyed after the program is finished, no auxiliary storage would be used to store them. This can save some overhead.

The following program segment first checks whether the data file exists in QTEMP; if it does, then delete it and create a new one in QTEMP; if not then go straight to the create file step. The data is copied to the file created in QTEMP so that another program can be run using this file. This kind of arrangement eliminates the record locking problem.

```
PGM
  .
  .
CHKOBJ LIB(QTEMP/file)
MONMSG MSGID(CPF9801) EXEC(GOTO label)
DLTF FILE(QTEMP/file)
label: CPYF FROMFILE(file) TOFILE(QTEMP/file)
           MBROPT(*ADD) +
   CRTFILE(*YES)
CALL PGM(program)
  .
  .
ENDPGM
```

Tip

Use QTEMP to store any temporary objects for your application.

5.1.4. How to Create a Library

A library can be created by using the Create Library (CRTLIB) command. In the CRTLIB command only the library name is compulsory; the other parts are optional.

The following is the syntax of the CRTLIB command:

```
CRTLIB LIB(library name) TYPE(library type) +
   AUT(authority) +
      TEXT(text descriptions)
```

Remember never to name a user library starting with the letter Q. The system would regard it as a system library in that case. The potential problem arises when you do a generic search for an object through all the system libraries; the user libraries named with the first letter Q would also be searched, thus wasting time and resources. On the other hand, when you do a search for a specific object through all the user libraries, the one you named with first letter Q would be omitted, so there is a chance of missing the desired object if it is in that user library.

In the CRTLIB command, the TYPE parameter can have either *PROD (production) or *TEST (test) as a value. As mentioned above, the difference between a production library and a test library is that the data files in a production library would not be updated when the program is running at debug mode, so the data files in a production library are protected. But bear in mind that the protection of the data in a production library is against update only; data records may still be deleted when the program is running at debug mode. In addition, this protection is valid on database files only; other data objects like data areas and data queues would still be updated.

Tip

Use CRTLIB to create a library.

The library, once created, is stored as part of the AS/400 internal system, and you will find it in the system library QSYS when you run the Work with Object (WRKOBJ) command:

```
WRKOBJ library-name
```

However, the created library is not really being stored in the QSYS system library. It is just the referencing method for any library when you run the WRKOBJ command on the AS/400.

5.1.5. Authority to a Library

Another very important parameter in the CRTLIB command is the Authority parameter, see Figure 5.3. The possible values for this parameter include:

Object Authority	Operational Authority	Management Authority	Existence Authority	Data Management Authority
*ALL	Yes	Yes	Yes	Read, Add, Update, Delete
*CHANGE	Yes	—	—	Read, Add, Update, Delete
*USE	Yes	—	—	Read Only
*EXCLUDE	No	No	No	No

Figure 5.3. Authority cross-referencing table.

1. *ALL

   The user can have all kinds of object operational authority, object management authority, and data management authority, which include deleting the library and any objects in the library in addition to changing the contents of the data objects. The user can also change the authority to the library and perform any other basic functions on the objects. However, the user cannot change the ownership of the library.

2. *CHANGE

   The user can add, change, or delete data records from database files and perform other basic functions on the objects in the library. Change authority allows the user to have object operational authority and data management authority on all objects in the library unless the authority to any particular object in the library is explicitly specified separately.

3. *USE

   The user can only have object operational authority and read authority on the object, which include displaying object descriptions and reading the contents of the object but not being allowed to add, change, or delete any information from the object. The *USE authority to a library also includes placing the library onto the library list, searching for an object in the library, displaying the contents of the library, and saving the library onto any magnetic media.

4. *EXCLUDE

This option prevents any user from accessing the object unless you specifically grant them the authority separately. This is the highest level of protection of the objects in your library.

5.1.6. Work with Library

You can use the Work with Library (WRKLIB) command to perform any update functions on the library, the library description, and any objects in the library for which the user has authorization.

The command syntax is:

```
WRKLIB library-name
```

Following are the options (functions) you can perform upon the library specified:

2 — change
3 — copy
4 — delete
5 — display
6 — print
8 — display library descriptions
9 — save
10 — restore
11 — save changed objects
12 — work with objects
14 — clear

You can change the library type and the text description by using option 2. Choose option 3 when you want to copy the library's contents to a new library. Use option 4 to delete the whole library. Use option 5 to display the list of objects contained in the library. Option 8 displays the library descriptions.

Type a 2 at the option bar when you want to change the library descriptions. The Change Library (CHGLIB) display menu comes up and then you can change the parameters you want to change.

Rather than using option 3 on the Work with Library display menu to copy the objects and place them into another library, you can accomplish the same task by using the Copy Library (CPYLIB) command:

```
CPYLIB FROMLIB(from-library-name) TOLIB(to-library-name)
```

This command also checks if the library in the TOLIB parameter exists already; if not, the system creates the library before any copy function takes place.

To clear or delete a library, you can invoke the Clear Library (CLRLIB) or Delete Library (DLTLIB) functions by choosing the appropriate options from the Work with Library menu. However, you can also run these two commands without getting into the Work with Library menu:

```
CLRLIB LIB(library-name)
```

and

```
DLTLIB LIB(library-name)
```

However, to delete a specific library, your user profile must have the object existence authority and object operational authority to the library and the object existence authority to the objects in the library.

In the case that your user profile has object existence and object operational authority to the library and the object existence authority to some but not all objects within the library, then those objects for which you have no existence authority would remain in the library after the delete library command was run, and the entire library would not be deleted. What you can do is get the object existence authority granted and then you can either delete each individual object by using the Delete Object command if the number of objects is not too great, or just run the Delete Library command again.

On the other hand, if your user profile has no object existence authority to the library at all, then even though you have the neccessary authority to delete the objects within the library, the Delete command cannot delete anything at all.

Another thing to bear in mind is that when the specified library is still on the library list of any active job on the system, you cannot delete the library.

Tip

Before you delete a library, run the WRKOBJLCK command to see if the library is being used by any other users.

Also, if the library you want to delete is specified as one of those libraries in the system value QUSRLIBL, you should take the deleted library name out of this system value as well; otherwise, when a new job is started in the system, the operating system would try to look for the deleted library. It would return an error message to the system operator message queue, since the deleted library is no longer on the system, and the job would not be started.

Tip

Use the CHGSYSVAL command to remove the deleted library from the system value QUSRLIBL.

5.1.7. Accessing an Object in a Library

There are two ways of accessing an object on the AS/400:

1. By using Qualified Name
   If the object name is qualified, it means that the library for the named object is specified.

   When the object name and library name are specified, the system would go directly to that library to search for the named object. The advantage of this is that the named library does not need to be on the library list, and the system can go straight to that library to access the specified object. In general, this is more efficient than scanning through the whole library list (i.e., using the second method below).

   When any command wants to locate any object by its qualified name, its OBJ parameter should always include the library name:

   ```
   PGM

   .

   .

   CHKOBJ OBJ(library name/object name) OBJTYPE(*FILE)

   .

   .

   ENDPGM
   ```

   And in some other cases, in the appropriate parameters:

   ```
   PGM

   .

   .

   CPYF FROMFILE(library name/object name)
   TOFILE(........)
   ```

.
.
.
```
ENDPGM
```

Tip

Using a qualified name means the object name also includes
the library name.

---

2. By using Library List

When a job is active on the system, it always has a library
list associated with it. The library list is the search path for
the objects you want. The library list resides in the main
memory during the lifetime of the job. Each time you enter
a system command or call a program, the system searches
through the library list for the objects required by the command or program.

When the object name is not qualified (meaning that the
library is not specified), the system searches through the library list to find the named object. The system searches
through the libraries from the top to the bottom in order of
occurrence until an object with the same name and type is
found.

In case there is more than one object having the same
name and type in these libraries, you would always get the
object that was found first. One thing you should bear in
mind is that if the library containing the expected object is
not in the library list, you would not be able to find the object at all. Therefore, it is very important that the pertinent
library is added to the library list before you run any program that refers to it.

In the searching process, any objects with the same name
but different object type would be bypassed.

You can specify the predefined value *LIBL when you
want to locate an object by library list:

```
WRKOBJ OBJ(*LIBL/object-name)
```

or just omit the library name in the above statement:

```
WRKOBJ OBJ(object-name)
```

The advantage of using a library list is that we can run the
same application program on different data without changing the application program.

For example, we can have two departments using the same set of application programs. Their database files can be separate and placed into two libraries. We can add the data library for the first department to the library list on the top of that of the second department. Then we run the application for the first department. When we want to run the application programs for the second department, we can just remove the data library of the first department from the library list. Running our application this way not only allows the data to be separate but also eliminates the need to accommodate the multidepartment situation in the software.

Tip

When you specify *LIBL or blank in the library parameter of any command, it searches for the object by library list.

5.1.8. Parts of a Library List

The library list can be divided into four parts:

1. System part
   The system part of the library list includes the libraries that contain the system commands, programs, and other system objects needed for system tasks. For example, QSYS, QUSRSYS, QSYS2, and QHLPSYS are the system libraries shipped by IBM.
2. Product libraries
   The product libraries are used to support system utilities or serve other purposes. At most, two product libraries can be included in the library list. The product libraries are placed between the system libraries and the user libraries so that the product commands and programs can be located more quickly than the user programs.
3. Current library
   The current library is the library where the created object is placed. You can specify any user library or General Purpose Library (QGPL) as the current library. If no current library is specified in the current job, then any created object would be placed in the QGPL. You can specify the current library by the Change Current Library (CHGCURLIB) command:

```
CHGCURLIB LIB(library-name)
```

Besides using the CHGCURLIB command you can also specify the current library in the user profile or in the Submit Job (SBMJ) command.

You can refer to the current library using the predefined value *CURLIB in your programs and commands.

4. User part

The user part of the library list contains libraries other than those described above (system libraries, product libraries, and the current library).

Figure 5.4 is the order of occurrence of the four parts in a library list.

Library List

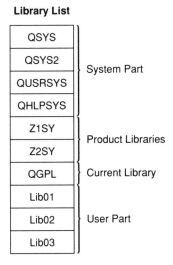

Figure 5.4. Order of occurrence in a library list.

5.1.9. Work with Library List

You can add and remove library list entries using the Edit Library List (EDTLIBL) command:

```
EDTLIBL
```

You can type the library names to the blanks to add libraries to the library list, or space over the library names to remove the libraries from the list. The sequence numbers determine their order of occurrence in the library list.

We can use a Display Library List (DSPLIBL) command to list all the libraries in the library list:

```
DSPLIBL
```

When we set up the library list for any job, we should consider the system performance to be an important issue.

The first thing we should keep in mind is that the library list be kept as short as possible, since a long library list would degrade system performance. The second thing we should think about is that libraries that are used most frequently should be placed on the top of the list so that it will take less time to find the frequently used objects.

The system values QSYSLIBL and QUSRLIBL contain the library lists that will be fetched into the initial library list of any new jobs. QSYSLIBL contains the libraries for the system part of the library list and QUSRLIBL contains the libraries for the user part of the library list. You can find out what these libraries are by using a Display System Value (DSPSYSVAL) command:

```
DSPSYSVAL SYSVAL(QSYSLIBL)
```

and

```
DSPSYSVAL SYSVAL(QUSRLIBL)
```

To change the library lists contained in the system value QUSRLIBL, we could use the Change System Value (CHGSYSVAL) command.

We can add to or remove library list entries from the library list in one single command using the Change Library List (CHGLIBL). This command is an alternative to the EDTLIBL command. The following statement shows how the library list can be changed using the CHGLIBL command:

```
CHGLIBL LIBL(the list of library names)
```

For example, if we have the following libraries in the library list:

QSYS
QSYS2
QUSRSYS
QGPL
QTEMP
LIB1
LIB2

and we run a CHGLIBL command:

```
CHGLIBL LIBL(LIB3 LIB4)
```

then the library list would become:

QSYS
QSYS2
QUSRSYS
LIB3
LIB4

That is to say, the system part would remain unchanged.

The effect of the CHGLIBL command only lasts for the lifetime of the job, or until the user changes the library list again.

Tip

The CHGLIBL command provides an alternative to the EDTLIBL command.

You can add one single library list entry to the library list using the Add Library List Entry (ADDLIBLE) command. You can specify where to place the library list entry with the POSITION parameter. For example, you can place the library list entry at the top of the user part as follows:

```
ADDLIBLE library-name *FIRST
```

or you can place the library list entry at the bottom of the user part as follows:

```
ADDLIBLE library-name *LAST
```

or you can place the library list entry immediately above another library as follows:

```
ADDLIBLE library-name POSITION(*BEFORE library-name)
```

You can remove a library list entry from the library list by using the Remove Library List Entry (RMVLIBLE) command:

```
RMVLIBLE library-name
```

Tip

ADDLIBLE and RMVLIBLE commands handle one single library at a time.

If you want to change the user part of the library list, you can use the Change Library List (CHGLIBL) command, Add Library List Entry (ADDLIBLE) command, or Edit Library List (EDTLIBL) command.

The commands discussed above, like CHGLIBL, ADDLIBLE, and RMVLIBLE, can all be coded in your CL programs and run by batch.

When you work with a library list, remember the following rules:

1. The library list specified in the system values QSYSLIBL and QUSRLIBL is overridden by the library list specified in the user profile or the parameter in the SBMJOB command.
2. The library list specified in the user profile or the parameter in the SBMJOB command is overridden by the library list specified by the CHGLIBL, ADDLIBLE, and RMVLIBLE commands after the job has become active.

When you create a batch job by submitting one to a job queue, you can always specify the initial library list for the submitted job in the initial library list parameter of the Submit Job (SBMJOB) command. This library list subsequently replaces the system values and becomes the initial library list of the batch job until it is changed again by any other library list commands.

In summary, for every job active on the system, the initial library list is fetched from the system values QSYSLIBL and QUSRLIBL, and this initial library list is subsequently replaced by the library list specified in the initial library list (INLLIBL) parameter, either in the Submit Job command if it is a batch job or as specified in the job description if it is an interactive job. Later on, you can override this in your program using the CHGLIBL, ADDLIBLE, or RMVLIBLE commands.

Tip

A library list in the user profile or the SBMJOB command overrides the library list in the system values QSYSLIBL and QUSRLIBL. Use the CHGLIBL, ADDLIBLE, and EDTLIBL commands to override the ones in the user profile or the SBMJOB command.

5.2. Object and Object Management

5.2.1. Object Type

On the AS/400, each object is identified by its object name and the object type, which is a very important attribute of the object.

The object type is a classification of entity that encapsulates a set of characteristics representing the object's standard behavior and properties. Each object type has its unique purpose of existence, and a different set of commands and common attributes associated with each object type.

On the AS/400 system, a terminal and a tape drive belong to two totally different object types; however, in some other operating systems both can belong to the same type. The set of commands that would perform on a tape device would definitely not work on terminals.

It is generally recognized that the AS/400 is a very user-friendly operating system. The truth is that the operating system performs some functions automatically on the objects behind the scenes, and a majority of these functions are transparent to the users. These functions are built-in functions implemented at the operating system or LIC level to guarantee that the object is handled in a consistent and proper manner.

The following functions are the built-in functions performed on the objects.

5.2.1.1. Object Type Verification

Each time a system command is requested to perform an action on an object, the system checks whether the object has the correct object type for the command before any action is performed on the object.

For example, before a Clear Physical File Member (CLRPFM) command is performed on an object, the system checks if the object specified is really a physical file member. If the object specified is not a physical file member the system does not perform the requested action; an error message is returned. This is done at the operating system level, and the programmer does not need to implement this in the program.

5.2.1.2. Object Authority Verification

Each time a system command is requested to perform an action on an object, the system also checks whether the user has the appropriate authority on the command and the object before any action is performed.

Using the example above, when you run the Clear Physical File Member (CLRPFM) command on an object, the system first checks whether the user has the permission to execute the command and, if so, it further checks whether the user has the authority to the object. If the user has both, the action is performed on the object. This is done at the operating system level and the programmer does not need to implement this in the program.

Figure 5.3 (shown earlier) is the cross-reference table summarizing the different authorities on the objects for the different values of the object authority.

We have already encountered several terms including object operational authority and object management authority. Now we will look into this further.

Object operational authority is the authority to display the object description.

A user who is given object operational authority to a library is allowed to display the object description for the library. These descriptions may include all the parameters you specified when you created the library.

Besides object operational authority, each object has the set of authority called object management authority. Object management authority is the authority to grant or revoke the authority to the object and the authority to rename the object. So if you have the object management authority to a library, you are allowed to change the other users' authority to the library, and also you can rename the library.

Data management authorities include read, add, update and delete authority to any data objects in a library. In the case where a user is allowed read authority only but no other authority, the user can run a program that only reads records from the data objects, but is not allowed to delete, update, or add any records to the data objects.

Tip

The authorities to any object include: object operational, object management, object existence, and data management.

Whenever you try to access an object, the system first checks your authority to the library that contains the object. Then it checks your authority to the specified object.

Therefore, even though the authority to an object is *CHANGE or *USE, you still cannot access the object if your authority to the library that contains the object is *EXCLUDE. In the case where the authority to the library is *USE and the authority to the objects is *CHANGE, you would be permitted to have the object operational authority and the data management authority on the objects.

The object authority can be granted by the Grant Object Authority command (GRTOBJAUT) or revoked by the Revoke Object Authority (RVKOBJAUT) command as followes:

```
GRTOBJAUT OBJ(object-name) OBJTYPE(object-type) +
   USER(*public) AUT(*USE)

RVKOBJAUT OBJ(object-name) OBJTYPE(object-type) +
   USER(*public) AUT(*EXCLUDE)
```

Each object belongs to an owner.

Usually the owner of an object is the user profile that creates it. However, you can change the object owner of an object by the Change Object Owner (CHGOBJOWN) command. The following statement shows you the syntax of the command:

```
CHGOBJOWN OBJ(object-name) OBJTYPE(object-type) +
   NEWOWN(user) CUROWNAUT(*SAME)
```

5.2.1.3. Object Locking Management

The system checks on the locking status of the object automatically whenever a user requests to update the contents of the object.

For example, if the object is already allocated by another user with the Exclusive but Allow Read (*EXCLRD) mode, then no other users would be able to update the contents of the object. If someone now wants to allocate the object with the Shared for Update (*SHRUPD) mode, the system would return with an error message. This is done at the system level and the programmer does not need to implement this object lock-checking routine in his program.

5.2.2. Object Descriptions

The system keeps detailed information for each object and this information is called Object Descriptions (object type is *OBJD).

The information included in the object descriptions are:

- The object name
- Library name
- Object type
- Object size
- Created date and time
- User who created the object
- User who owns the object
- Date last used
- Storage size
  etc.

You can either display this information on-screen using the Display Object Descriptions (DSPOBJD) command or retrieve these internal attributes using the Retrieve Object Descriptions (RTVOBJD) function in your CL programs.

The following program segment shows you how to retrieve the object owner from the object descriptions using the RTVOBJD command:

```
PGM
DCL VAR(&OWNER) TYPE(*CHAR) LEN(10)
    .
    .
    .
CHKOBJ OBJ(file name) OBJTYPE(*FILE)
MONMSG MSGID(CPF9801) EXEC(GOTO EXIT)
RTVOBJD OBJ(file name) OBJTYP(*FILE) +
   OWNER(&OWNER)
    .
    .
    .
EXIT: ENDPGM
```

5.2.3. Other Functions That Operate on an Object

Besides the built-in functions mentioned above, there are some other functions that can be applied to an object. They have to be called by the user on an as needed basis.

The functions which can be performed on the objects by the user on an as needed basis include the following.

5.2.3.1. Rename Object

The system command to rename an object on the AS/400 is the Rename Object (RNMOBJ) command.

You can rename an object as follows:

```
RNMOBJ OBJ(object-name) OBJTYP(object-type) +
  NEWOBJ(new-object-name)
```

Tip

You should check for the existence of the object to be renamed before you rename it. This guarantees that the RNMOBJ command will not fail.

There are some special objects that you cannot rename, for example, the system library QSYS that are shipped by IBM, the temporary library QTEMP created and associated with each active job on the system, user profiles, workstation message queues, system operator message queue (QSYSOPR), controller descriptions, device descriptions, line descriptions, and so forth.

Output queues cannot be renamed if they still have any output files in them.

You may notice that you do not need to specify the library for the renamed object; the reason is that you are supposed to put the renamed object in the same library. The renamed object would always remain in the same library. If you want to place it in a different library, you can rename it first and then do a move object (MOVOBJ) to another library.

To rename an object, you need the object management authority on the object and the read and update authority on the library.

When you are about to rename an object, you need to pay special attention to the dependencies of the object. For example, before you rename a physical file, you need to check if some logical files depend on the physical file, and whether the file would be accessed in any programs. To check on the database dependencies, you can do a Display Data Base Relation (DSPDBR) command for the physical-logical files relationships. If you do not change the name of the object to the new name in your program, the object won't be found when the program is run.

5.2.3.2. Delete Object

There is no delete command that can delete all kinds of object types on the system; the reason is that the system does some verification checking, as mentioned above, at the system level before the deletion is performed. Since this kind of checking is unique for each object type, we do not have the luxury of a delete command that can apply to all object types.

Therefore there are different delete commands for different object types. For example, to delete physical and logical files there is a Delete File (DLTF) command, and to delete a program there is the Delete Program (DLTPGM) command.

Before any physical file is deleted, the system checks to see if there are any logical files dependent on it and, if so, the system does not delete the physical file until all the logical files dependent on it are deleted first.

To delete a display file, the system checks to see if there are some HLL programs using it and, if so, the system does not perform the deletion until all programs using the specified display file are deleted as well.

The following line deletes a physical file:

```
DLTF file-name
```

To delete a program, there is the Delete Program (DLTPGM) command:

```
DLTPGM program-name
```

To perform deletion of the object, you need to have object existence authority on the object and the read authority of the library.

Tip

Make sure the object to be deleted is on the library list if you refer to it by library list.

5.2.3.3. Create Duplicate Object

The system command Create Duplicate Object (CRTDUPOBJ) creates a duplicate copy of an existing object.

The following statement creates a duplicate object of file type from an existing object:

```
CRTDUPOBJ OBJ(original object) FROMLIB(library) +
   OBJTYP(object type) +
   TOLIB(library) NEWOBJ(new object name)
```

The duplicate object has the same object type and object authority as the original object. The duplicate object is placed in the same storage pool as the original object as well, and the user who runs the CRTDUPOBJ command is the new owner of the duplicate object.

In order to duplicate an object in a library, you need to have the object operational authority, object management authority, and read authority on the original object, the object operational authority on the library in which the original object resides, and the object operational authority and add authority on the library in which the duplicate object going to be placed.

Most of the time you will want to create duplicate copies of files and programs, but there are certain objects you cannot duplicate because if the object is allowed to be duplicated the operating system would be confused. These special objects include library names, data queue names, user profiles, controller descriptions, device descriptions and line descriptions, and so forth. In other cases, like job queue, message queue, and output queue, you can only duplicate the descriptions (i.e., definitions) of these queues but not create another physical object with the same name. You cannot create a duplicate job queue with the same contents as the original job queue.

5.2.3.4. Move Object

The system command Move Object (MOVOBJ) can move one object from one library to another. But to run this command you need the object management authority to the object, the read and delete authority to the library in which the object resides, and the add authority to the library to which you want the object moved.

```
MOVOBJ OBJ(object name) OBJTYP(object type) +
   TOLIB(new library)
```

The statement above moves the object as specified to another library.

You can use this command to move a majority of the object types from one library to another, but there are some object types that you cannot move, for example, libraries, user profiles, workstation message queues, system operator message queue (QSYSOPR), controller descriptions, device descriptions and line descriptions, and so forth. You can move an output queue from one library to another only when the output queue has no output files in it.

Like those Delete Object commands, you have to be careful when you want to move an object from one library to another. You should check the object dependencies (e.g., database relations) first for a physical file before moving it since there could be some logical files dependent on the existence of the physical file, and there could be some HLL programs accessing the physical file as well. In another case, subsystem descriptions would refer to special objects like job queues, message queues, output queues, and so forth, and if you move a job queue to another library you need to change the subsystem descriptions as well.

5.2.3.5. Allocate and Deallocate Object

The purpose of object allocation is to ensure data integrity, referential integrity, and concurrency.

    The data in the object is protected by the Allocate Object (ALCOBJ) command so that any data in the object is not lost or altered unexpectedly. There are five allocation modes that you can specify on the object when you execute the ALCOBJ command; they are:

1. Shared for Read (*SHRRD) mode
   When an object is allocated with *SHRRD mode, you can read from the object and at the same time you share the object with the other users. There are no restrictions on how the other users may use the object; the other users can read, add, update, or delete data from the object while you are reading from it, or even impose an Exclusive mode on the object as well. This mode has the least level of protection on the object.
   The syntax is:
   ```
   ALCOBJ OBJ(object-name object-type *SHRRD)
   ```
2. Shared for Update (*SHRUPD) mode
   When you allocate an object with the Shared for Update mode, you want yourself and other users to be allowed to read or change the contents of the object concurrently.
   The syntax is:
   ```
   ALCOBJ OBJ(object-name object-type *SHRUPD)
   ```
3. Shared No Update (*SHRNUP) mode
   When you allocate an object with the Shared No Update mode, you and the other users can only read data from the object but are not allowed to change the contents of the object.
   The syntax is:
   ```
   ALCOBJ OBJ(object-name object-type *SHRNUP)
   ```

4. Exclusive allow Read (*EXCLRD) mode

   When you allocate an object with the Exclusive allow Read mode, you prohibit other users from changing the contents of the object. You can do anything to the allocated object, but the other users can only read data from it.

   The syntax is:

   ```
   ALCOBJ OBJ(object-name object-type *EXCLRD)
   ```

5. Exclusive (*EXCL) mode

   When you allocate an object with the Exclusive mode, only you can read and change an object; no other users can read data or change the contents of the object. This mode has the highest level of protection of the object.

   The syntax is:

   ```
   ALCOBJ OBJ(object-name object-type *EXCL)
   ```

We can basically allocate every kind of object type on the system, for example, libraries, database files, programs, subsystem descriptions, message queues, data areas, data queues, and so forth. On one hand, we can allocate these objects as needed; on the other hand, the objects to be accessed by other system commands are checked automatically by the system at the operating system level for any object locks before these commands can operate on the allocated object. For example, user A can allocate a file with Shared for Update (*SHRUPD) mode for data entry purposes, and user B issues the command to allocate the object with Shared for Read (*SHRRD) mode in order to print a listing of the data records in the file. Then the operating system checks on the object-locking status at the time user B issues the ALCOBJ command to make sure that user B is allowed to allocate the object at the specific mode wanted.

In order to allocate an object you must have object operational, object existence, and object management authority on the object. One thing to bear in mind is that having a library allocated does not mean having the objects in it allocated as well. You need to allocate the objects in the library separately. Even though you have allocated a library with the Shared No Update (*SHRNUP) mode, the objects in the library can still be updated by you and other users if you do not impose the ALCOBJ command on the objects.

Tip

When you allocate a library even with an *EXCLRD mode, other users cannot add or delete objects from that library, but they can still update objects in that library.

You can code the ALCOBJ command in your CL program and change the lock status at any time necessary during the duration of the program.

You should also implement the MONMSG command in case your program fails to allocate the object. We will examine the MONMSG command in a later chapter, but basically the MONMSG command serves as an error trap in the CL program, for example,

```
ALCOBJ OBJ(file *FILE SHRNUP)
MONMSG MSGID(......) EXEC(GOTO EXIT)
 .
 .
 .

EXIT: ENDPGM
```

where the MONMSG command makes the program branch to the statement labeled EXIT when the ALCOBJ command fails.

You can run a Deallocate Object (DLCOBJ) command on the allocated object at the end of the job. However, the DLCOBJ command is optional since the allocated object is deallocated automatically at the end of the routing step anyway.

5.2.3.6. Check for Existence

It is good programming practice to check the object for existence before any desired command is to be performed on it.

You can check the object for existence using the Check Object (CHKOBJ) command, which, if the object does not exist, returns an error message. This command not only examines the object's existence but also checks whether you have the authority to perform any operations on it.

The CHKOBJ command has the following syntax:

```
CHKOBJ OBJ(object name) OBJTYP(object-type)
```

If the CHKOBJ command detects that the object does not exist or you have no authority to perform operations on it, it would send an error message to your program message queue. You can implement the MONMSG command in case the program fails to find the object. Here the MONMSG command serves as an error trap in the CL program, for example,

```
CHKOBJ OBJ(file) OBJTYP(*FILE)
MONMSG MSGID(......) EXEC(GOTO EXIT)
 .
 .
 .
```

```
EXIT: actions
   .
   .
   .
ENDPGM
```

where the MONMSG command makes the program branch to the statement labeled EXIT when the CHKOBJ command fails.

The six commands discussed above manage objects by user on an as needed basis.

Command Summary

CRTLIB	Create a Library
WRKOBJ	Work with Object
WRKLIB	Work with Library
CPYLIB	Copy Library
CLRLIB	Clear Library
DLTLIB	Delete Library
WRKOBJLCK	Work with Object Lock
CHGCURLIB	Change Current Library
EDTLIBL	Edit Library List
DSPLIBL	Display Library List
CHGLIBL	Change Library List
ADDLIBLE	Add Library List Entry
RMVLIBLE	Remove Library List Entry
GRTOBJAUT	Grant Object Authority
RVKOBJAUT	Revoke Object Authority
CHGOBJOWN	Change Object Owner
DSPOBJD	Display Object Descriptions
RTVOBJD	Retrieve Object Descriptions
RNMOBJ	Rename Object
CRTDUPOBJ	Create Duplicate Object
MOVOBJ	Move Object
ALCOBJ	Allocate Object
DLCOBJ	Deallocate Object
CHKOBJ	Check Object for Existence
DLTF	Delete File
DLTPGM	Delete Program

Exercises

5.1. What is the difference between a production library and a test library?

5.2. What are the characteristics of the library QTEMP?

5.3. Explain the two different ways of accessing an object.

5.4. What is a library list? What are the parts of a library list?

5.5. What information is contained in the object descriptions?

5.6. What are the object authorities?

Jobs

Actions are performed by the system through the execution of jobs. A subsystem is the environment in which jobs are executed. The AS/400 has a unique concept of work and its management. Therefore, we will look at these concepts before any CL commands are explained. It is very important that you understand the concepts before you learn to run any commands and write programs using these commands.

This chapter introduces the concept of Job and Work Management. On the AS/400 there are many types of jobs that have diversified purposes. We will look at how a job is run on the AS/400. Also, the details of the concepts of subsystem and subsystem descriptions will be examined in detail.

6.1. Definitions

6.1.1. What Is a Job?

By definition, a job is a single, identifiable sequence of processing actions that represent a single use of the system. Therefore, every piece of work that runs in a subsystem is called a job.

A subsystem is a single, predefined operating environment in which the system coordinates the work flow and resources. You can always create a subsystem whose attributes determine how work is to be done under that particular environment, and you can always run a job under that environment (subsystem) after it is defined.

For example, you can define a subsystem that handles all the workstation jobs and is totally dedicated to handle the interactions between the machine and the users. On the other hand, you can define a special environment to handle the printing jobs, which would take care of the printers and the spooled files.

To summarize, a job is a sequence of actions to be processed in a subsystem, and a subsystem is an operating environment under which work is done in a predefined manner.

6.1.2. Types of Jobs

On the AS/400 system, there are several types of jobs:

6.1.2.1. Interactive Job

An interactive job starts when the user signs on to the machine and lasts until the user signs off. A job is created by the system to interactively react to the user's responses and thus is called an interactive job.

6.1.2.2. Batch Job

A job is called a batch job when a series of actions are submitted to a job queue for execution in one single job stream. The batch job is started when the job submitted to the job queue is selected from the queue and run in a subsystem. A batch job can be submitted by an interactive job, by another batch job, or by a communication job. However, the difference between a communication batch job and an ordinary batch job is that a communication batch job can be started by a communication program from another machine and does not need to be submitted to a job queue.

Tip

An interactive job needs the user's interactions. A batch job, on the other hand, does not need any user intervention at all.

6.1.2.3. Spooling job

A spooling job can be for input or output.

In an input spooling job, a system program called a reader transfers jobs from the input devices such as a diskette or database file. For output spooling, the job puts the output from a program into a spooled file, and later the spooled file can be written to an external device such as a printer.

6.1.2.4. Autostart Job

An autostart job is always associated with a subsystem, and whenever the subsystem is started the autostart job is started as well. An autostart job can be programed to carry out either repetitive work or one-time work. On the AS/400 system the work is done in storage pools, which are logical divisions of the main storage. We can also define a specific working environment, called a subsystem, which executes the jobs using the resources of the storage pools. The advantage of this arrangement is that we can group similar jobs with common characteristics and place them into the same operating environment (subsystem) so that they can be controlled collectively and independently of the other jobs.

For example, we may want to end all interactive jobs and dedicate the whole machine to one batch job (e.g., the month-end process) for performance purposes. Then we just end the subsystem for interactive jobs and leave the batch job subsystem running.

In some cases we can decrease the storage pool size allocated to the subsystem dedicated for batch jobs so that the interactive jobs have a much larger storage pool to improve the response time, if neccessary.

6.2. Job Name

Every job has a unique job name for the purpose of control and identification. The qualified job name consists of three parts:

- Job name
- User name
- Job number

For an interactive job, the job name is the device name of the workstation and for a batch job it is the 10-character name you specify in the Submit Job (SBMJOB) command when you submit the job to the job queue.

For an interactive job the user name is the user profile you use when you sign on to the workstation, and for a batch job it is the user profile with which the batch job is submitted to run.

The job number is a 6-digit numeric assigned by the system. For example, if user profile SMITH signs on to a workstation with device name DSP12 then the interactive job the user has started would have a job number

```
DSP12/SMITH/987347
```

where 987347 is a system-assigned number.

User SMITH can now submit a batch job to a job queue using the SBMJOB command, and he can specify the job name to be test1 in the Submit Job (SBMJOB) command. The syntax of the SBMJOB command is:

```
SBMJOB CMD(CALL PGM(program-name)) JOB(job-name)
```

If the job is submitted successfully, the system returns with a message that a batch job with job number

```
823772/SMITH/test1
```

is submitted to the job queue, where 823772 is a system-assigned number.

You can always use the Retrieve Job Attributes (RTVJOBA) function to retrieve the qualified job name for the current job in the CL program as shown:

```
PGM
DCL VAR(&JOBNAME) TYPE(*CHAR) LEN(10)
DCL VAR(&USER) TYPE(*CHAR) LEN(10)
DCL VAR(&JOBNUM) TYPE(*CHAR) LEN(10)
 .
 .
 .
RTVJOBA JOB(&JOBNAME) USER(&USER) NBR(&JOBNUM)
 .
 .
 .
ENDPGM
```

The function RTVJOBA retrieves the three components of a qualified job name separately and returns their values into the three separate program variables.

6.3. Job Descriptions

6.3.1. Definitions

A job description is a collection of parameters that control the job when it is started in the subsystem.

As mentioned earlier, every piece of work run in a subsystem is called a job. Each job is a single, identifiable sequence of processing actions that represent a single use of the system. Every job to be started on the system must use a job description.

The advantage of using a job description is that once it is defined you can use it anywhere just by referring to the job description name whenever you want to start a job. It eliminates the trouble of defining the same working environmental parameters for every job you want to start.

6.3.2. How to Create Job Descriptions

A job description is created using the Create Job Description (CRTJOBD) command. Following are the more important parameters of the Create Job Description command:

The Job Queue (JOBQ) parameter is the name of a defined job queue in which the job will be placed if it is a batch job.

When you do a Work with Job Queue (WRKJOBQ) command:

```
WRKJOBQ job-queue-name
```

the display would include the following columns:

column 1 — option for user input
column 2 — job name
column 3 — user
column 4 — number
column 5 — job priority
column 6 — job status

Column 5 is the priority of the jobs, and this priority determines which job would go into the storage pool for execution first. Priority 1 is the highest priority and priorities with a larger integer would have lower priority, but you can change the job priority of a batch job using the Change Job (CHGJOB) command if you have job control special authority.

The Job Priority (JOBPTY) parameter determines the priority of the job on the job queue.

The Output Priority (OUTPTY) parameter determines the priority of the spooled output file created by the job. The priorities range from 1 to 9, with priority 1 the highest priority. However, if the spooled files are already created by the job, you can change the output priority of the spooled files using the Change Spooled File Attribute (CHGSPLFA) command:

```
CHGSPLFA FILE(*SELECT) OUTPTY(1)
```

Print Device (PRTDEV) is the default printer the spooled files would go to.

Output Queue (OUTQ) is the default output queue to which the spooled output files of the job are to be sent.

The User (USER) parameter is the user profile name the job takes when it is started.

The Routing Data (RTGDTA) parameter of the job description is the data used to compare with the subsystem's routing entries and determine which routing program will run.

The Request Data (RQSDTA) parameter of the job description is where you specify your command to run.

Initial Library List (INLLIBL) is the user part of the initial library list for the job.

The Hold on Job Queue (HOLD) parameter determines whether a job submitted to a job queue is to be held until it is explicitly released by the user.

You can change the parameters of a job description using the Change Job Description (CHGJOBD) command. Use the Delete Job Description (DLTJOBD) command to delete a job description.

The program segment in Figure 6.1 illustrates how you can code the Change Job Description (CHGJOBD) command in your CL program. The program prompts the user to enter an option on a menu and upon receiving the reply from the user it calls different programs depending on the option number entered by the user. At the time we submit the job for the option chosen we may need to alter the parameters for the job description; in this case it is the routing data that needs to be changed, and we make the change using the CHGJOBD command.

In your CL program, you can retrieve the job attributes with the Retrieve Job Attributes (RTVJOBA) command. There are about 39 job attributes that are involved with each job. Some of the more important attributes include:

- Job name
- User name

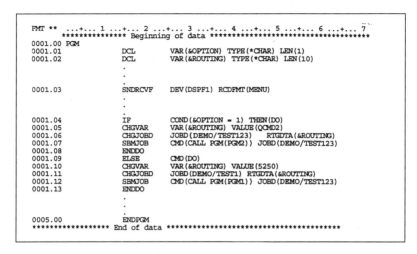

```
FMT **    ...+... 1 ...+... 2 ...+... 3 ...+... 4 ...+... 5 ...+... 6 ...+... 7
          ************** Beginning of data ************************************
0001.00 PGM
0001.01              DCL            VAR(&OPTION) TYPE(*CHAR) LEN(1)
0001.02              DCL            VAR(&ROUTING) TYPE(*CHAR) LEN(10)
                                    .
                                    .
                                    .
0001.03              SNDRCVF        DEV(DSPF1) RCDFMT(MENU)
                                    .
                                    .
                                    .
0001.04              IF             COND(&OPTION = 1) THEN(DO)
0001.05              CHGVAR         VAR(&ROUTING) VALUE(QCMD2)
0001.06              CHGJOBD        JOBD(DEMO/TEST123)    RTGDTA(&ROUTING)
0001.07              SBMJOB         CMD(CALL PGM(PGM2)) JOBD(DEMO/TEST123)
0001.08              ENDDO
0001.09              ELSE           CMD(DO)
0001.10              CHGVAR         VAR(&ROUTING) VALUE(5250)
0001.11              CHGJOBD        JOBD(DEMO/TEST1) RTGDTA(&ROUTING)
0001.12              SBMJOB         CMD(CALL PGM(PGM1)) JOBD(DEMO/TEST123)
0001.13              ENDDO
                                    .
                                    .
                                    .
0005.00              ENDPGM
          ****************** End of data ***************************************
```

Figure 6.1. Change Job Description

- Job number
- Message logging level
- Output queue
- Job switches
- Job running priority
- Time slice
- System library list
- User library list
  etc.

The values for these parameters are placed in the predefined program variables.

6.4. Subsystem and Subsystem Descriptions

Before we go into any details of the mechanism of job handling, we should know a little bit more about subsystem and subsystem descriptions.

6.4.1. Definitions

A subsystem is a single, predefined operating environment in which the system does its work.

There are a number of subsystems that operate independently and separately from one another on the system. During the work being done the system resources are shared among all the subsystems. There are a whole set of attributes associated with each subsystem; these attributes are called Subsystem Descriptions. Subsystem Descriptions are a specific type of object on the AS/400 system; they define how jobs are run in that particular subsystem.

These attributes include:

1. Operational attributes, for instance, maximum number of jobs allowed in subsystem
2. Pool definitions, which designate which system storage pool to use
3. Autostart job entries
4. Workstation name entries
5. Workstation type entries
6. Job queue entries, which define job queues to be attached to this subsystem
7. Routing entries
8. Communications entries

6.4.2. How to Create a Subsystem Description

You can create a subsystem description using the Create Subsystem Descriptions (CRTSBSD) command. The following shows you how to create a subsystem description using the CRTSBSD command:

```
CRTSBSD SBSD(library/subsystem-description) +
    POOLS((4 1000 3) (2 1000 1)) MAXJOBS(3)
```

Once the subsystem is created, it can be started by the Start Subsystem (STRSBS) command:

```
STRSBS SBSD(library/subsystem-descriptions)
```

To stop the subsystem from running, use the ENDSBS (End Subsystem) command:

```
ENDSBS SBSD(subsystem-descriptions)
```

but you should check if there are any jobs still running in the subsystem before you end it.

The commands above can be coded in CL program and run by batch.

You can always change the subsystem descriptions using the Change Subsystem Descriptions (CHGSBSD) command, if you have the special authority to do so.

6.4.3. How to Create a Class

After the subsystem description is created, we can create the class for the subsystem. The class is created by the CRTCLS (Create Class) command:

```
CRTCLS CLS(library/class-name)
```

After the class is created, you can refer to it when you add a routing entry to the subsystem description later.

A class is a set of parameters that control the running environment of a job. These parameters include:

Running Priority (RUNPTY) — is a number between 1 and 99 with 1 as the highest priority. It determines which job is given machine resources when more than one job are requesting system resources. You can always use the Change Job (CHGJOB) command to change the priority parameter of your job:

```
CHGJOB RUNPTY(10)
```

Time Slice (TIMESLICE) — specifies the processor time, in milliseconds, allowed for a job before any other waiting jobs are given the resources to run. As mentioned before, while a job is waiting for data or a program from the auxiliary storage, or waiting for a response from the user, it can be displaced from the main storage so that the resources can be given to another job to run. The time slice parameter determines how long a job will wait before it is displaced. You can always use the Change Job (CHGJOB) command to change the time slice parameter of your job:

```
CHGJOB TIMESLICE(50000)
```

Purge (PURGE) — indicates whether the job's Process Access Group (PAG), which includes all the objects that are unique to the job, would be purged from the main storage after the end of the time slice. After the PAG's objects are purged it would be placed in auxiliary storage. The job's routing step is also a member object in the PAG.

Default maximum Wait time (DFTWAIT) — specifies how long the job would be held up by the system in seconds.

Maximum Processing Time (CPUTIME) — specifies the maximum amount of time a job can run in the system in seconds.

Maximum Temporary Storage (MAXTMPSTG) — specifies the maximum amount of temporary auxiliary storage a job can allocate.

Most of these parameters limit the uses of system resources so that no one single program can impair system performance because of errors.

Usually we would give higher priorities to interactive jobs than to batch jobs. Therefore, we can create a class with higher priority and specify it in the routing step for the interactive subsystem.

You can use the Change Job (CHGJOB) command to change the class attributes mentioned above for a job's routing step, but the changes are only effective during the lifetime of the job.

6.4.4. Subsystem Attributes

Subsystem attributes define the overall subsystem characteristics. This includes the storage pool definitions, and their sizes and activity levels. In the CRTSBSD statement above, we have designated the storage pools to this subsystem within the CRTSBSD command:

```
POOLS((4 1000 3) (2 1000 1))
```

and, after this is done, if we display the pool definitions using the Work with Subsystem (WRKSBS) command we should see:

Pool ID	Storage Size (K)	Activity Level
2	1000	1
4	1000	3

Whenever the subsystem is started, the system attempts to allocate the storage size as requested in the subsystem description. But if the system cannot allocate all the requested storage, it allocates as much storage as is available. For example, if there are only 1500 KB of storage available, then 1000 KB would be allocated to the first storage pool and the remaining 500 KB would be allocated to the second storage pool, although it has requested 1000 KB.

One thing to bear in mind is that the storage pools the system has allocated would decrease the size of the base storage pool (system pool with identifier 2) until the amount of storage available to the base storage pool has already reached the minimum base pool size as defined in the system value (QBASPOOL).

The activity level for a pool specifies the maximum number of jobs that can run at the same time in that storage pool. Once the maximum activity level is reached, any other jobs requesting storage will be put in a queue and their job status will become ineligible until one of the jobs in the pool gives up its use of the storage. Then the job in the queue can become active again.

The storage pool does not need to be large enough to contain the program you want to run because the operating system would manage the transfer of program and data into and out of the storage pool. If the data that the program requested is already loaded in main storage, it can be referred to by a routing step. If the data is not yet loaded, then the needed data would be loaded into main storage and some other data would be displaced out of main storage. The system manages the control of this process at the machine level.

There can be more than one job active in a subsystem due to the "time-sharing" concept that, while one job is waiting for data from auxiliary storage or for a response from the user, it can give up the usage of the storage pool, and during that period of time, no matter how small it is, another job can run using the resources the waiting job has just released.

Besides the pool definitions, the subsystem attributes also include maximum number of jobs allowed in the subsystem, sign-on display file, authority, and a text description of the subsystem.

6.4.5. Work Entries

Work entries are defined to identify the sources from which jobs can be started for running in that subsystem. Work entries include autostart job entry, workstation entry, job queue entry, and communications entry.

6.4.5.1. Autostart Job Entry

An autostart job entry specifies a job that will be automatically started when the subsystem is started. Usually an autostart job is used to do the initialization work for an application. Once defined in the subsystem description, the job is automatically started each time the subsystem is started.

6.4.5.2. Workstation Job Entry

A workstation job entry specifies one or a group of workstations from which interactive jobs can be started. Once defined in a subsystem description, the job is processed whenever a workstation user signs on.

6.4.5.3. Job Queue Entry

Each job queue entry specifies one of the job queues from which the subsystem can select batch jobs.

6.4.5.4. Communication Entry

A communication entry specifies one or a group of communication device descriptions by name or by type, or a remote location name from which communication jobs can be started. The job is processed when the subsystem receives a communication program start request from a remote system.

You can add these work entries to the subsystem description with the following commands:

Add Autostart Job Entry (ADDAJE) command
Add Work Station Entry (ADDWSE) command
Add Job Queue Entry (ADDJOBQE) command
Add Communications Entry (ADDCMNE) command

You can also change or remove the work entries using the following commands:

Change Autostart Job Entry (CHGAJE)
Remove Autostart Job Entry (RMVAJE)
Change Work Station Entry (CHGWSE)
Remove Work Station Entry (RMVWSE)
Change Job Queue Entry (CHGJOBQE)
Remove Job Queue Entry (RMVJOBQE)
Change Communications Entry (CHGCMNE)
Remove Communications Entry (RMVCMNE)

6.4.6. Routing Entries

A routing entry is a description of how a job is to be started.

After the subsystem descriptions and class are created, you can use the Add Routing Entry (ADDRTGE) command to add routing entries to the subsystem descriptions:

```
ADDRTGE SBSD(library/subsystem-descriptions) +
   SEQNBR(sequence-number) +
      CMPVAL(*ANY) +
         PGM(program-name)
```

Every job is processed in a subsystem as one or more consecutive routing steps. A routing step is the processing done as a result of calling the program as specified in the subsystem description's routing entry.

A routing entry contains values that control the selection of programs to start the routing step and that include sequence number, comparison value, starting position, program name, class, and storage pool identifier.

The sequence number identifies the routing entry, determines the order in which the routing entries are scanned, and is also used as an identifier of the routing entry. The comparison value specifies the data to be compared with routing data to decide which routing entry to use.

The routing data is compared with the comparison value of each routing entry in the sequence number order until either a match is found, or there is no match. When a routing entry is matched with a comparison value that matches the routing data, a routing step is started and the program as specified in that routing entry is called. The control values such as run priority, time slice, wait time, maximum CPU time, and maximum temporary storage that are defined in the class associated with the routing entry are used for the routing step in the storage pool specified in the routing entry. On the AS/400 system, a class is an object.

Whenever a job is started, the right routing entry is selected by comparison of the routing data and the comparison value for each routing entry until a match is found, and if no match is found the job is aborted. The routing data of the job to be run is extracted from the job description associated with the job; you can also supply the routing data when you submit a batch job to a job queue using the SBMJOB command. We will look at how a job is started in a later section.

Figure 6.2 shows you the routing entries of a subsystem description.

The display in Figure 6.2 includes the following columns:

column 1 — option bar for user input
column 2 — sequence number
column 3 — program name
column 4 — library name
column 5 — compare value
column 6 — starting position

```
                        Display Routing Entries

     Subsystem description:    QINTER          Status:    ACTIVE

     Type options, press Enter.
       5=Display details

                                                                        Start
     Opt   Seq Nbr    Program        Library       Compare Value        Pos
       _      10      QCMD           QSYS          'QCMDI'               1
       _      20      QCMD           QSYS          'QS36'                1
       _      40      QCMD           QSYS          '5250'                1
       _     700      QCL            QSYS          'QCMD38'              1
       _    9999      QCMD           QSYS          *ANY



                                                                       Bottom
     F3=Exit    F9=Display all detailed descriptions    F12=Cancel
```

Figure 6.2. Subsystem routing entries display.

Column 2 is the sequence number of the routing entries. This sequence number tells the subsystem the order in which routing entries are to be searched for a routing data match. Therefore if your routing data is QCMDI the search ends with routing entry 10. However, if your routing data does not match any one of the compare values, which range from QCMDI to QCMD38, then the last routing entry is used since its comparison value is *ANY, which means it can match with anything.

One thing to bear in mind is that when you define routing entries you should order them so that the entry most likely to be compared and matched would come first, because this can reduce the search time.

Once a match is found, the program as specified in the Program column is called to start the job. Runtime environmental parameters as defined in the class associated with that routing entry are used for the job.

Figure 6.3 summarizes the different attributes of subsystem descriptions.

6.5. How a Job Is Started in a Subsystem

An interactive job comes into existence when a user signs on to the system. A batch job comes into existence when a user does a SBMJOB. However, the mechanism behind the scene is more complicated than that.

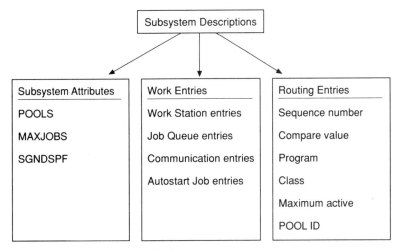

Figure 6.3. Subsystem descriptions.

6.5.1. Routing Data

When a job is started, the subsystem that is starting the job has to decide the program the job will run by scanning through the routing entries until it finds a match for the routing data. This process is called "routing" the job. However, a job can have multiple routing steps, and the following are the cases when a job happens to have alternative routing steps:

1. The job is rerouted by using the Reroute Job (RRTJOB) command in a program
2. The execution of the RETURN command in a called program
3. The execution of the Transfer Job (TFRJOB) command in a program

If you do a Reroute Job (RRTJOB) command, you are starting a new job routing step in the same subsystem. Transferring a job using the TFRJOB command does the same thing. In both cases, when the subsystem reroutes the job, all the file overrides are removed, all objects that have been allocated would be deallocated, and files are closed. However, the job attributes would remain the same. The purpose of rerouting is to change the processing attributes since you are using a new routing entry to process the routing step.

An interactive job or batch job can be transferred to another subsystem by using the RRTJOB or TFRJOB commands.

The routing data of a job can be specified in the following ways:

1. in the Job Descriptions (JOBD) of the job
2. in the Request Data (RTGDTA) parameter of a Submit Job (SBMJOB) command
3. in the Request Data (RTGDTA) parameter of a Reroute Job (RRTJOB) or Transfer Job (TFRJOB) command

Figure 6.4 shows how an interactive job can be started on the system.

Figure 6.5 shows how a batch job can be started on the system.

6.5.2. System Objects and Job

Once a job has started to run, the system assigns a storage pool to it. So long as the job remains active, it would remain in the assigned storage pool until the end of the job. Jobs that are active would from time to time use system objects, which include the following:

- Data areas
- File override information
- Device files
- Logical files
- Physical files
- Program variables
- Application codes
- System codes
- Queues (job queues, message queues, output queues)
- Open data path
  etc.

When the job needs to use these objects, they have to be in main storage. If they are not already in main storage they have to be read into main storage from disk. These system objects can be shared by more than one job. For example, a system program that is called by two different jobs always resides in main storage as one single copy; the second job using it does not need to make a copy of it.

However, the program variables and all job-related objects are not shared among those jobs.

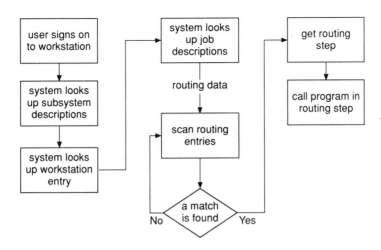

Figure 6.4. How an interactive job is started.

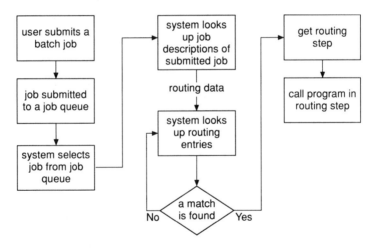

Figure 6.5. How a batch job is started.

In summary, objects that are shared by all jobs include: data areas, system code, user programs, database files. Objects that are unique to each job include: record buffers, file override information, open data path, program variables, local data area, and so forth. They are collectively called Process Access Group (PAG). The PAG that is unique to each job must be in the main storage as long as the job is active.

6.5.3. Library List and Job

For every job running on the AS/400 there is always a library list associated with it. A library list is simply a list of library names through which the system searches for the required objects.

For example, if the program wants to open a file, then the system would search for the file from the topmost library on the library list to the bottom one. If there is more than one file having the same name in the library list, the first one it comes across is selected. Therefore in our CL programs we should arrange the libraries in the proper order; otherwise unexpected results would occur.

You can add a library to the library list using the Add Library List Entry (ADDLIBLE) command. For example, when you want to add the library to the top of the user part of the library list:

```
ADDLIBLE library-name *FIRST
```

The parameter *FIRST indicates that the library will be placed at the top of the user part of the library list.

The library list can be divided into two parts: the system part and the user part. The system part includes the system libraries. The user part includes all the user libraries. The system part is always at the top of the user part so that the system commands and other system objects can be accessed more efficiently and quickly.

6.6. Interactive Jobs

An interactive job starts when a user signs on to a workstation and lasts until the user signs off. We have already seen how an interactive job starts in Figure 6.4, which shows the activities leading to the startup of a routing step, displaying the initial menu for a user profile, and executing an initial program for that user profile.

When a user signs on to a workstation, the system looks up the work station entries for the subsystem QINTER to determine which Job Description (JOBD) to use for this interactive job to be started. Usually the job description for the workstation entries is *USRPRF; that means use the job description of the user profile (*USRPRF).

You can always display the workstation entries by using the Work with Subsystem (WRKSBS) command.

For every user profile there is an attached job description. If you do a Display User Profile (DSPUSRPRF) command you will see the job description on the second screen. To find out what information is contained in the job description you can do a Display Job

Description (DSPJOBD). The display invoked by the DSPJOBD command shows you the details of the job description. The routing data will be on the second screen. When the job is started, the subsystem tries to find a match for the routing data by scanning through all the routing entries sequentially for the subsystem. The routing entries for the subsystem, which can be found out by using the Work with Subsystem (WRKSBS) command, were seen in Figure 6.2 as an example.

The compare value of the routing entry is compared with the routing data of the job description. If the routing data matches the compare value for the routing entry, the subsystem selects that routing step to start. The routing program for the routing step starts to run and it will load the initial menu and call the initial program as specified in the user profile.

The program QCMD is a system program that invokes the system Command Entry panel; it serves as an interface between the user and the operating system. You can enter a user program to the Initial program parameter in your user profile so that every time you sign on to the workstation this program is automatically loaded into the main storage and run. The advantage of making QCMD the initial program is that it will bring you to the Command Entry panel where you can enter any system commands or call any user-written programs over there if you wish.

6.7. Batch Job, Output Queue, and Job Queue

The difference between an interactive job and a batch job is that a batch job is the result of placing an entry in a job queue instead of signing on to a workstation. We have already seen how a batch job can be started.

Before we add a job queue entry to a subsystem description, the job queue must have been created.

6.7.1. How to Create a Job Queue

You can create a job queue by using the Create Job Queue (CRTJOBQ) command. This command creates an object of type *JOBQ and places it in a library; you can add the job queue entry, using the newly created job queue, to any subsystem description.

The parameters that you can specify in the CRTJOBQ command include:

Operator Controlled (OPRCTL)

It indicates whether any users can control the job queue and its contents if that user has the job control authority. If the parameter is *YES, then only the system operator can have control of that job queue.

Authority to Check (AUTCHK)

It indicates whether only the owner of the job queue has the authority to check the contents of the job queue.

Text Description (TEXT)

It is a text description of the job queue.

6.7.2. Add Job Queue Entry

The Add Job Queue Entry (ADDJOBQE) command can be used to add the reference of using a particular job queue to a subsystem description. You can do this as follows:

```
ADDJOBQE SBSD(subsystem description) JOBQ(job queue) +
    SEQNBR(number)
```

You can neither add a job queue entry to a subsystem description nor remove a job queue entry from a subsystem description while the subsystem is still active. Make sure the subsystem is not active when you add the job queue entry to the subsystem description. If the subsystem is still active, you need to end the subsystem using the End Subsystem (ENDSBS) command.

The sequence number should be unique for each job queue entry in a subsystem description. You cannot add a job queue entry with a sequence number that already exists in that subsystem description. The use of the sequence number is to determine how jobs are being selected to run from a job queue.

Suppose we have several job queue entries defined for a subsystem; the subsystem would then select jobs from the job queue with the lowest sequence number. The sequence number is the number you assign to the job queue entry using the ADDJOBQE command; its value ranges from 1 to 9999. Number 1 is the lowest sequence number. The subsystem would continue to select jobs to run from the job queue with the lowest sequence numbers until it reaches its maximum activity level or if there are no more jobs in the job queue. Then the subsystem would select jobs from the job queue with the second lowest sequence number. This selection process would continue until there are no more job entries on the job queue or the subsystem has reached its maximum activity level, which is specified in the Maximum Jobs Allowed parameter in the subsystem description. Figure 6.6 illustrates how the sequence number determines how jobs are selected from a job queue.

For example, assume the maximum activity level for the subsystem is 3 jobs and we have three job queue entries defined for this subsystem description. Each one of the job queues has maximum activity level *NOMAX, say. Job Queue JOBQ1 has sequence number 10, Job Queue JOBQ2 has sequence number 11, and Job Queue JOBQ3 has sequence number 12. Now nine batch jobs are submitted to the job queues JOBQ1, JOBQ2, and JOBQ3, respectively, three jobs for each job queue. Suppose we have named the submitted jobs JOB1, JOB2, and JOB3, which are submitted to job queue JOBQ1; JOB4, JOB5, and JOB6, submitted to job queue JOBQ2; and JOB7, JOB8, and JOB9, submitted to job queue JOBQ3. Then, all three jobs submitted to job queue JOBQ1, namely, JOB1, JOB2, and JOB3, will be selected and run first since job queue JOBQ1's sequence number is the lowest.

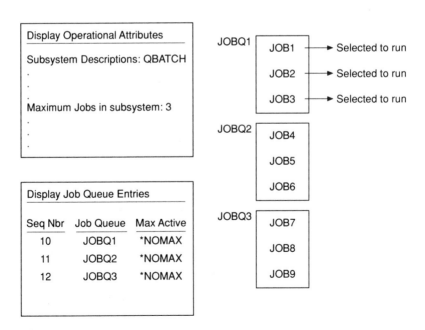

Figure 6.6.

However, if the maximum activity for each job queue is changed to 1 now, then JOB1 from job queue JOBQ1, JOB4 from job queue JOBQ2, and JOB7 from job queue JOBQ3 will be selected to run first. See Figure 6.7.

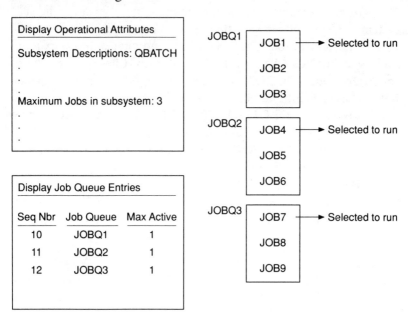

Figure 6.7.

When a subsystem is started it will try to allocate all of its job queues. But this allocation may fail if the job queue does not exist, cannot be locked, or is already allocated to another subsystem. Bear in mind that a job queue can exist independent of any subsystem, and if you want to use a job queue you can refer to it by adding it as a job queue entry in the subsystem description. Of course, you can add the same job queue to more than one subsystem description as a job queue entry. More than one subsystem description can refer to the same job queue but only one active subsystem can use the job queue as a source of batch jobs at any one time.

You can delete a job queue from the system without removing the job queue entry from the subsystem descriptions, and if that is the case, it would give you an error message when you start the subsystem. Jobs can be placed on the job queue even if the subsystem is not started, but once the subsystem is started it starts to select jobs to run from the job queues.

Not all jobs in the job queue would be processed even if the subsystem is started, since there are two status conditions for jobs already submitted to the job queue: Released (RLS) and On Hold (HLD). If the submitted job is put on hold, it will remain in the job queue until it is released explicitly.

6.7.3. Work with Job Queue

You can find out whether your jobs are still being held in the queue by using the Work with Job Queue command:

```
WRKJOBQ job-queue-name
```

If the subsystem is ended before all the jobs are processed, the jobs would still remain in the job queue until the subsystem is started again or until another subsystem allocates the same job queue; then those jobs in the job queue are selected to run again.

If another subsystem has already started and is waiting for the same job queue while the original subsystem is inactive, the second subsystem will allocate the same job queue and select a job from the job queue to run. Basically it is very similar to an interactive job: the subsystem looks up the job description of the batch job to find out the routing data. Then it compares the routing data with the comparison value of each routing step until a match is found. If no match is found, the job is aborted. If a match is found, then the matching routing step would be started and the program as specified in that routing step is called.

You can supply the routing data for the submitted job in the SBMJOB command, and if that is the case, the routing data in the job description will be overridden by that value.

6.7.4. Output Queue

Output queues are objects of type *OUTQ on the AS/400 system. It is a place to hold the output spooled files created by jobs. The operating system automatically creates an output queue for every printer device created. However, you can always create an output queue for your own purposes.

6.7.4.1. How to Create an Output Queue

You can create an output queue by using the Create Output Queue (CRTOUTQ) command. The CRTOUTQ command creates an output queue; the parameters for this command include:

Order of files on queue (SEQ) — specifies the order of the spooled files on the output queue. There are two options: First-In-First-Out (*FIFO) and by Job Number (*JOBNBR). If you specify Job Number, the spooled files are sorted by the date and time the job entered the system.

Text description (TEXT) — you can enter a 50-character text.

Display any file (DSPDTA) — specifies whether someone who has the permission to read the output queue can also display the contents of the output files on the output queue.

Job Separators (JOBSEP) — specifies the number of separators placed at the beginning of the output files for each job with files on the output queue. The separator contains information such as job name, user name, job number, and the date and time the job entered the system.

Operator Controlled (OPRCTL) — specifies whether someone who has job control authority can also control the contents of the output queue.

Authority to Check (AUTCHK) — specifies whether the commands that check the requester's authority to the output queue would also check for ownership authority and data authority as well.

Authority (AUT) — specifies the authority granted to the users.

6.7.4.2. How Output Queue Is Used

Submitted jobs wait in a job queue until the subsystem selects the job from the job queue. The job may produce output files that are placed in an output queue. This process is called spooling.

A writer, which is a system device, selects the output files on an output queue for writing to a printer device.

When you submit a batch job to the job queue using the SBMJOB command, you can always specify the output queue for the job at the OUTQ parameter:

```
SBMJOB CMD(call pgm(program name)) JOB(job name) +
  OUTQ(output queue)
```

Then the output files, which may include the spooled files and the job log, are placed in the output queue. If you do not specify the output queue, it will send the spooled files to the default output queue as specified in the job description.

The default output queue name in the job description is over-ridden if you specify an output queue name of your choice. You can use the Work with Output Queue (WRKOUTQ) command to ma-nipulate the spooled files on the queue:

```
WRKOUTQ output-queue-name
```

6.7.4.3. Other Commands Related to Output Queue

There are several other commands you can use to handle output queue:

Change Output Queue (CHGOUTQ) — you can use this com-mand to change the parameters of the output queue, for ex-ample, if you want to change the sorting sequence of the spooled files from *FIFO to *JOBNBR:

```
CHGOUTQ OUTQ(output queue name) SEQ(*JOBNBR)
```

Clear Output Queue (CLROUTQ) — if you want to delete all spooled files on the output queue:

```
CLROUTQ OUTQ(output queue name)
```

Hold Output Queue (HLDOUTQ) — if you want to hold all the spooled files from printing:

```
HLDOUTQ OUTQ(output queue name)
```

This command changes the status of the output queue to HLD. All the spooled files on the output queue can still be RLS (Released) while the output queue is on hold, and none of the released spooled files will go to the printer device if the output queue is still on hold.

Release Output Queue (RLSOUTQ) — this command releases the output queue if the queue was put on hold.

```
RLSOUTQ OUTQ(output queue name)
```

Delete Output Queue (DLTOUTQ) — this command deletes the object from the system.

6.7.5. How to Submit a Batch Job

You can use the Submit Job (SBMJOB) command to submit a batch job to a job queue. You can do that at the system command line or code it in your CL programs. You can specify the following param-eters in the SBMJOB command:

Job Name (JOB) — you can specify a 10-character name for the job.

Job Description (JOBD) — if you do not specify then the Job Description of your user profile would be used.

Job Queue (JOBQ) — if you do not specify then the Job Queue in your job description would be used.

Job Priority (JOBPTY) — it is the priority of the job on the job queue. If you do not specify then the Job Priority in your user profile's job description would be used.

Output Priority (OUTPTY) — it is the priority of your output files on the output queue. If you do not specify then the Output Priority in your user profile's Job Description would be used.

Routing Data (RTGDTA) — it is the data you supply and will be used for comparison with the comparison value of the routing step.

Initial Library List (INLLIBL) — it is the user part of the library list you want to specify.

Hold on Job Queue (HOLD) — it indicates whether you want the job being put on hold after it is submitted to the Job Queue.

You can submit another batch job to a job queue while it is still running in the system. You can pass parameters to the submitted job by using local data areas, program variables and constants, messages and so forth.

When the job queue name (JOBQ) is not supplied in the Submit Job (SBMJOB) command, the job is placed on the job queue named in the job description. You can always use the Work with Submitted Jobs (WRKSBMJOB) command to display jobs submitted.

Tips

How do you force a submitted job to run at a different priority or time slice? Remember that the SBMJOB command cannot accept override values for priority and time slice.

One way to do this is with the CHGJOB command.

Another way is to create a new class object where you assign the new priority or time slice, then add a routing entry to the subsystem using the new class object. From now on, include the routing data when you submit a job with the SBMJOB command.

6.7.6. Other Commands Related to Jobs

The WRKSBMJOB command shows you the jobs submitted and their status.

Status JOBQ means the job is still waiting in the job queue. Status ACTIVE means the job is now running in the storage pool. Status OUTQ means the job is completed and its output files have been put on the output queue.

You can switch to another job queue for the submitted job. One way to do it is to put a 2 at the option bar and then specify the new job queue name at the command line. Another way to move a submitted job to another job queue is to use the Change Job (CHGJOB) command.

You can always implement the Change Job (CHGJOB) command in your CL program. For instance, you can change the message logging level of the current job as follows:

```
CHGJOB LOG(4 0 *SECLVL) LOGCLPGM(*YES)
```

There is a command called Delay Job (DLYJOB) that can put the current job on hold until the resume time specified or after a period of time has elapsed. The following statement shows you how to implement the DLYJOB command:

```
DLYJOB RSMTIME(2300)
```

6.8. Storage Pool Size and Performance

We can check out the storage pool size by using the Work with System Status (WRKSYSSTS) command. On the AS/400 system, the main storage can be divided into logical allocations called storage pools. System pool with identifier 1 is always the machine storage pool, which is used for machine and operating system programs; no other user jobs would run in this pool. There is a minimum machine pool size when you configure the system and that minimum size totally depends on the model of your machine. In addition to the minimum pool size, we also need to calculate the additional main storage needed for each communication line, protocol, and controller. Of course, as the number of communication lines increases we need to readjust this figure. The minimum machine pool size is contained as a system value that can be displayed using the DSPSYSVAL command:

```
DSPSYSVAL SYSVAL(QMCHPOOL)
```

System pool with identifier 2 is always the base storage pool, which contains all unassigned main storage on the system. Unassigned means not required by the machine pool or by another active subsystem. This storage pool can be shared between subsystems and most of the time the base storage pool is used for batch jobs and other miscellaneous operating system functions. The minimum pool size for the base storage pool is contained as a system value that can be displayed using the DSPSYSVAL command:

```
DSPSYSVAL SYSVAL(QBASPOOL)
```

System pools with identifiers 3, 4, 5, and higher are allocated for active subsystems, and as many as 14 such additional storage pools can be allocated.

Each storage pool has a size and an activity level. The activity level determines the maximum number of jobs that can share the pool at any time. By limiting the number of jobs sharing the storage pool, you can give each job enough room to run efficiently. Although the primary purpose of the activity level is to avoid having too many jobs compete for main storage, it also limits the number of jobs sharing the processor at the same time.

The AS/400 automatically adjusts pool sizes and activity levels via the system value QPFRADJ, which you can use to control the way AS/400 adjusts these values.

Sometimes people may think that the CPU usage has the greatest effect on performance, but this may not be the case. After changing storage pools and the maximum active jobs parameters, we may have a relatively decent response time even though the CPU usage is running at 95 percent or above. Therefore, we have to look at a lot of factors and that should be the proper approach of performance tuning.

6.9. Work with Active Jobs

You can find out what jobs are now running on the system by using the Work with Active Jobs (WRKACTJOB) command.

The Work with Active Jobs display in Figure 6.8 shows the current status for every job running on the system.

column 1 — option bar for user input
column 2 — subsystem/job
column 3 — user
column 4 — type

```
                            Work with Active Jobs                    BRIAN
                                                          11/23/92  20:38:51
      CPU %:    13.0      Elapsed time:   00:00:03    Active jobs:   52

      Type options, press Enter.
        2=Change   3=Hold   4=End   5=Work with   6=Release   7=Display message
        8=Work with spooled files   13=Disconnect ...

      Opt  Subsystem/Job  User      Type  CPU %  Function       Status
           BATCH1         QSYS      SBS    .0                   DEQW
        _    SAVLIB       QSYSOPR   BCH    .1    CMD-SAVLIB     TAPW
        _    QDFTJOBD     SMITH     BCH   4.4    PGM-PGM001     RUN
        _  BDS            QSYS      SBS    .0                   DEQW
        _    QDFTJOBD     QSYSOPR   BCH    .0    PGM-PGM021     DEQW
        _    PRT01        QSYSOPR   BCH    .0    PGM-PRT023     DEQW
        _    SYS36        QSYSOPR   BCH    .0    PGM-S36P1      DEQW
        _  QPGMR          QSYS      SBS    .0                   DEQW
        _  QCMN           QSYS      SBS    .0                   DEQW
                                                                   More...
      Parameters or command
      ===>
      F3=Exit      F5=Refresh    F10=Restart statistics   F11=Display elapsed data
      F12=Cancel   F23=More options   F24=More keys
```

Figure 6.8. Work with Active Jobs display.

> column 5 — CPU %
> column 6 — function
> column 7 — status

The fourth column in the display is the job type, which indicates the type of job on the AS/400 system:

> BCH — batch job
> INT — interactive job
> WTR — spooling job
> SBS — subsystem monitor job

You can also find out which storage pool this job is running in; display the elapsed data by pressing the function key <F11>.

The last column in the Work with Active Jobs display is Status, indicating the current status of the job. Every job running on the AS/400 system can be in any one of the three status conditions:

1. Active

   When a job is active, it has been placed in the main storage and is doing work.

2. Wait

   When a job is waiting for some resource that is not available now, it is said to be in a wait state. There are two kinds of wait states: short wait and long wait. Short wait happens in the main storage and the job is waiting for a resource that is unavailable for less than 2 seconds. If the wait is longer than 2 seconds it will be changed to a long wait. The difference is that short wait does occupy an activity level but a long wait does not.

Tip

There are many kinds of waiting states, for example:
> waiting for the completion of an I/O
> waiting for the completion of a communication call
> waiting for the completion of a dequeue operation
> waiting for the input from a workstation
> waiting to try a read operation
> waiting for an event
> waiting for a lock
> waiting for a message
> waiting for output to a printer

Press the <HELP> key to find out the details.

---

3. Ineligible

   When a job becomes ineligible it means that the system cannot perform any more work at that time and the job has been displaced out of main storage. When a job becomes ineligible, it does not occupy any activity level. As mentioned above, the activity level for a storage pool is the maximum number of jobs that can run at the same time in that storage pool.

Command Summary

CRTSBSD	Create Subsystem Descriptions
STRSBS	Start Subsystem
ENDSBS	End Subsystem
CRTCLS	Create a Class
CHGJOB	Change Job Attributes
ADDRTGE	Add Routing Entries
CRTJOBD	Create Job Descriptions
CHGJOBD	Change Job Descriptions
WRKSBS	Work with Subsystems
ADDJOBQE	Add Job Queue Entries
WRKJOBQ	Work with Job Queue
SBMJOB	Submit Job
WRKSBMJOB	Work with Submitted Jobs

DLYJOB	Delay Job
CRTOUTQ	Create Output Queue
CHGOUTQ	Change Output Queue
CLROUTQ	Clear Output Queue
HLDOUTQ	Hold Output Queue
RLSOUTQ	Release Output Queue

Exercises

6.1. What components are in a job name?

6.2. What information is contained in the job descriptions?

6.3. What attributes are contained in subsystem descriptions?

6.4. What is a class?

6.5. Explain routing entries.

6.6. What is a job queue? What is an output queue?

6.7. What commands would you use to submit a batch job?

7

Interprogram Communication

This chapter introduces the different methods of communication between a CL program and another CL or HLL program. These methods may involve some special objects and concepts that you have not encountered in any previous chapters, for example, data area, data queue, and switches. Therefore we will first examine the characteristics of these objects before we discuss using them for interprogram communication.

7.1. Modular Programming

Modern software design employs the idea of modular design and programming. The idea of modular design suggests that a large program should be broken down into a number of smaller modules that accomplish different tasks. Therefore, instead of coding one big program, we now have several small programs that are called by the main program. Each individual module should have a purpose different from the others. This kind of software design makes it easier to maintain the software, and it becomes more reusable.

Figure 7.1 shows a structure chart of a program that employs modular design.

Communication between programs has become very important since it directly affects the efficiency and effectiveness of a system that employs modular design.

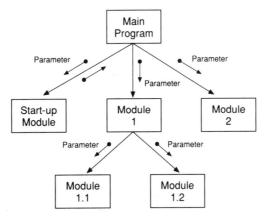

Figure 7.1. Modular design of programs.

7.2. Communication Between Programs

There are many ways to communicate between programs; we have different choices under different situations. Remember that there is no single best way for all situations. We can pass information to and from another program using:

- Parameter
- Data area
- Message
- Data queue
- Switch
- Database file

These will be examined in the following sections.

7.3. Using Parameters

7.3.1. Advantages and Disadvantages of Parameters

The advantage of using parameters is that it does not involve any other objects in the system besides the programs passing and receiving them. Parameters are stored in main memory; using parameters thus can save system resources, especially disk I/O. Figure 7.2 shows the objects needed for each kind of communication.

Type of Communication	Object Needed
Parameters	none
Data area	Data Area (*DTA, *LDA, *GDA, *PDA)
Messages	Message Queue (*MSGQ)
Data queue	Data Queue (*DTAQ)
Switch	Switch (00000000)
Database file	Database files

Figure 7.2. Objects needed for communications.

The disadvantage of using parameters is that you can only pass parameters to a program that is being called by the initiating program, and the receiving program must be running in batch mode as well. A job running in batch on the AS/400 is nothing like a DOS batch file. On the AS/400, the term "batch" should only be used in opposition to "interactive."

There is also a limitation on the number of parameters that can be passed to the receiving program. You can pass parameters to another program using the CALL or TFRCTL commands in your CL program. When you pass parameters in your CL program, make sure that the parameters defined in the calling program have the same data type and length as the parameters declared in the called program.

7.3.2. Passing Parameters in CALL Function

We implement the CALL command as follows.
Sending program:

```
PGM
DCL VAR(&A) TYPE(*DEC) LEN(10 2)
DCL VAR(&B) TYPE(*CHAR) LEN(5)
DCL VAR(&C) TYPE(*DEC) LEN(7 2)
CALL PGM(receiving-program) PARM(&A &B &C)
.
.
.
ENDPGM
```

Receiving program:

```
PGM PARM(&X &Y &Z)
```

```
DCL VAR(&X) TYPE(*DEC) LEN(10 2)
DCL VAR(&Y) TYPE(*CHAR) LEN(5)
DCL VAR(&Z) TYPE(*DEC) LEN(7 2)
 .
 .
 .
ENDPGM
```

When you use the CALL command to pass parameters, you need to specify in the CALL command the list of parameters you want to pass. In the receiving program, you need to specify the list of parameters that the called program is receiving. If the data types in the calling program and called program do not match, you will receive an error message. Therefore, if variable &A is defined as decimal of length 10, say, but the receiving variable &X is declared as character of length 10, then the value of the receiving variable &X will be unreadable by the program after the parameter is passed to the receiving program.

On the other hand, if variable &A is declared as character of length 10 and receiving variable &X is declared as decimal of length (10 0), then you will receive an error message when you run the program. If you rely on the value of &X for calculations in the program, unexpected results will occur.

Remember that in the two lists of parameters in the calling and called programs, the order of parameters must match. Therefore, in sending and receiving programs above, the value of variable &A is passed to variable named &X in the receiving program, &B is passed to &Y, and &C is passed to &Z. In CL programs, parameters are passed by the position in the parameter list, not by their names in the program.

Tip

Parameters are passed by the position in the parameter list.

7.3.3. Types of Parameters

Parameters that can be passed to another program can be:

- Program variables
- Character string constants
- Numeric constants
- Logical constants

Passing program variables as parameters is quite straightforward; the sending and receiving programs shown above demonstrate how to pass program variables as parameters.

The receiving program does not allocate any storage for the CL variables passed from the sending program as parameters; therefore, we do not need to return any variables passed as parameters back to the calling program. In fact, the value of these variables are already updated after control is returned to the calling program.

Tip

Parameters are stored in the main memory.

Decimal constants are passed as (15 5), that is, decimal of length 15 with 5 decimal positions in packed format (remember that all decimal variables are packed in CL).

Decimal constants are passed as follows in a CL program. Sending program:

```
PGM
CALL PGM(receiving-program) PARM(1234.56)
.
.
.
ENDPGM
```

Receiving program:

```
PGM PARM(&X)
DCL VAR(&X) TYPE(*DEC) LEN(15 5)
.
.
.
ENDPGM
```

The value of &X in the receiving program will be

```
'    1234.56000'.
```

However, if you declared variable &X as decimal (15 2) instead of (15 5), then you would get unexpected results. The value of &X is now

```
'    1234560.00'
```

If your program uses this variable for calculations you would get incorrect results.

If you want to pass a decimal constant in another format, decimal (15 2) say, instead of (15 5), you need to pass it in hexadecimal format. Decimal constant 1234.56 has become

X'000000000123456F' in hexadecimal format. The CALL command would look like this:

```
CALL PGM(receiving-program) PARM(X'000000000123456F')
```

The value of the receiving variable would be 1234.56.

If numeric constants are quoted in the CALL command, it is passed as a character string. On the other hand, if no quotes is specified, it is passed as a decimal variable of length (15 5).

If you pass a decimal constant to the receiving program where it is declared as a character string, the value of the receiving variable would become unreadable. If the lengths do not match in the sending and receiving programs, like the (15 5) and the (15 2) case above, an error may occur when you want to use it in the receiving program. As we have already seen above, when 1234.56 is passed to the receiving program its value becomes 1234560.00 instead, so if we use this constant for calculations we would get unexpected results.

You may encounter errors not only in the receiving program, but also in the sending program after control is returned.

If a character string constant is less than or equal to 32 bytes, then it is passed as 32 bytes. If it is greater than 32 bytes, then it will be passed as exactly the number of bytes as is. Therefore, if the character string constant you want to pass is greater than 32 bytes, you should declare its length as equal to or greater than its actual length to avoid truncation.

Logical constants are always passed as 32 bytes. However, only the first byte is used and the receiving program expects either a 1 or 0.

CL programs do not support floating point and binary data type. But you can use CL programs to receive floating point or binary data and pass the data in hexadecimal format to another HLL program like RPG or COBOL, which support the floating point or binary data type.

CL programs can pass parameters from and to other HLL programs such as RPG and COBOL as well.

The TFRCTL command is different from the CALL command in the following ways:

- Parameters to be passed must be CL variables, not constants.
- CL variables to be passed to another program must be received from another calling program.
- TFRCTL is only valid in batch mode within a CL program.

7.4. Using Data Areas

7.4.1. What Is a Data Area?

A data area is an object of type *DTAARA on the AS/400 system. Its use is mainly for the storage of information for asynchronous communication. Of course, you can run two or more programs concurrently, and each of them passes information to and from a data area, but strictly speaking this is not asynchronous communication. The real meaning of asynchronous communication is that one program is completed and the output of the first program is stored in an area, then the second program starts after the first one is completed and it retrieves the output of the first one from the data area, that is, there is always a time gap between the two programs. The second program gets the output of the first program by retrieving information from the data area.

A data area has no internal structure; you cannot define a data area with data fields in a record format, like the data structures in other HLL programs. Of course, you can always allocate some section of the data area for some particular data items, but these data items are only meaningful to your program. From the system's point of view, this division is meaningless to the operating system.

A data area contains small amounts of nonrepetitive information. Every time you want to store a single piece of information that does not have multiple occurrences, you can use a data area instead of a file.

One limitation of a data area is its limited size. The length of the data area, once decided, cannot be changed. Since a data area is for asynchronous communication, it is independent of the existence of any programs or jobs. It is stored in a library and can be accessed by any programs at any time unless it has been allocated by any one particular job for exclusive use. The advantage of using a data area is that it allows communication between two or more programs running at different times in different jobs. In most of the cases, data areas are used to:

1. Provide an area to pass information within a job, between two or more jobs running at the same time, or between two or more jobs running at different times.
2. Provide an area that can be updated frequently in order to store reference or control data for use within a job or between two or more jobs.
3. Provide an area to hold constant values for jobs running at different times.

7.4.2. How to Create a Data Area

Data areas are created by using the system command Create Data Area (CRTDTAARA). The data area, once created, would be stored in the library specified, and it will continue to exist until it is deleted from the library. The data area is created as follows:

```
CRTDTAARA DTAARA(library/data-area) TYPE(*CHAR)
```

Of course, you can code the CRTDTAARA command in your CL programs. The data area created above would be of type *CHAR, and its length would be 32 bytes, since you have not specified the length in the command. You can display the contents of the data area using the DSPDTAARA (Display Data Area) command; the contents is just blank space since the default value of the data area is blank if you do not specify any initial value in the CRTDTAARA command. You can specify the length of the data area by adding the length parameter to the CRTDTAARA command as follows:

```
CRTDTAARA DTAARA(library/data-area) TYPE(*CHAR) LEN(50)
```

You can also specify the initial value while you create the data area. You just add the value parameter to the command as follows:

```
CRTDTAARA DTAARA(library/data-area) TYPE(*CHAR) +
   LEN(50) VALUE(X)
```

When we create the data area, we can only initialize it from the first position of this data area and not from any other position in this area. But, of course, we can update the data area with those values at a later time. You can also create a data area of type decimal. You can specify the type as *DEC and give it a length while you create it. The following is an example to create a data area of type *DEC and length (9 2), with an initial value of 2.5:

```
CRTDTAARA DTAARA(library/data-area) TYPE(*DEC) +
   LEN(9 2) VALUE(2.5)
```

If you do not specify the length and initial value above, the system defaults to length (15 5) and 0 as the initial value. You can also create a data area of type *LGL:

```
CRTDTAARA DTAARA(library/data-area) TYPE(*LGL)
```

The default length of a logical data area is 1 and its initial value is 0.

Most of the time we create a character data area and assign different positions in the data area to store the logical values instead of creating several logical data areas. A data area created by the CRTDTAARA command is a library-specific object. We will need the DLTDTAARA (Delete Data Area) command to delete the data area once it is created.

Tip

A data area has no internal structure and its length and data type are determined when it is created.

7.4.3. Other Commands Related to Data Area

You delete an existing permanent data area as follows:

```
DLTDTAARA DTAARA(library/data-area)
```

The other commands that you can use in your CL programs to manipulate data areas include:

CHGDTAARA (Change Data Area)
RTVDTAARA (Retrieve from Data Area)

The CHGDTAARA statement below shows you how to update a data area. The syntax of the CHGDTAARA command is as follows:

```
CHGDTAARA DTAARA(data-area-name (1 20)) VALUE('hello!')
```

which updates the data area named from position 1 to position 20 with the character string of value 'hello!'.

You can update the contents of a data area with a program variable as well. For example, you can update the data area named from position 30 to 40 with the value in the variable &VAR1, say, in your CL program as shown here:

```
CHGDTAARA DTAARA(data-area-name (30 40)) VALUE(&VAR1)
```

In CL programs we can retrieve the information from the data area using the RTVDTAARA command. The RTVDTAARA command can retrieve the desired information from the data area and returns its values into a CL variable. Then you can work with the CL variables in any way you want. The RTVDTAARA command has the following syntax:

```
RTVDTAARA DTAARA(data-area-name (1 20)) RTNVAR(&TEMP)
```

The statement above retrieves the contents in the data area named from position 1 to 20 and returns its value to a variable named &TEMP. The variable &TEMP should be declared as character variable with length 20; otherwise truncation may occur.

You may use the DSPDTAARA (Display Data Area) command to display the contents in the data area but it is not a usual practice to use the display function in the batch mode.

Tip

Allocate the data area in your program when you want to update the contents in it.

7.4.4. Types of Data Area

Besides the permanent data area mentioned above there are some other special types of data area on the AS/400:

- Local Data Area (LDA)
- Group Data Area (GDA)
- Program Initialization Parameter data area (PIP)

7.4.4.1. Local Data Area

A local data area (an object of type *LDA) is created for each job running on the system. After the local data area is created, it can only be accessed by the current job, and no other jobs except jobs submitted by the current job can get access to it. This is the reason this type of data area is called a "local" data area. The data type of the local data area is always *CHAR and length 1024 bytes, with initial value blank.

You may try to delete the local data area using the DLTDTAARA command but you would find that a local data area cannot be deleted. The local data area associated with the current job will only be destroyed when the current job is ended.

Since a local data area is only accessible to the current job and no other jobs are able to access it, you do not need to use the Allocate Object (ALCOBJ) command on the local data area in your CL programs.

Bear in mind that a local data area is not a permanent object, it is not stored in any library, and it is always in main memory. Performance would be improved if a local data area is used instead of a permanent data area, since any program would need to do a disk I/O to access it.

You can use the CHGDTAARA and RTVDTAARA commands on the local data area and the %SST function to retrieve or update data on it as well.

When you update a local data area you need to specify the starting position and the length of the updating string. For example,

```
CHGDTAARA DTAARA(*LDA (1 5)) VALUE('hello!')
```

In the statement above, you use the CHGDTAARA command to update the local data area with the character string 'hello!' starting at its first position. You can also update the local data area with any CL variable defined in your program:

```
CHGDTAARA DTAARA(*LDA (1 5)) VALUE(&VAR1)
```

where &VAR1 is declared in your CL program as a variable.

You can retrieve the contents of the local data area using the RTVDTAARA command:

```
RTVDTAARA DTAARA(*LDA (1 15)) RTNVAR(&VAR1)
```

The RTVDTAARA command above retrieves the contents in the data area from the first position to position 15, and returns its value to a CL variable &VAR1.

You can also use the %SST function combined with the CHGVAR function to extract a portion of the local data area and return its value into any CL variable.

```
CHGVAR VAR(&A) VALUE(%SST(*LDA 1 15))
```

In the statement above, the substring function extracts from the local data area a string 15 characters long and assigns its value to a CL variable named &A. In your CL program, you have to make sure that the data type of the receiving variable &A is also defined as character in this case. If you declared the data type as decimal you will receive an error message when you run the program. But in case the local data area contains only digits (0–9), then the contents are converted into numeric value and no error message is received.

In the following statement the substring function is combined with the CHGVAR function to update the local data area with the specific value:

```
CHGVAR VAR(%SST(*LDA 1 15)) VALUE('hello there!')
```

A local data area exists across the routing step boundary only; as mentioned earlier, it is only accessible to the current job or any batch jobs submitted by the current job. The local data area of the submitting job is copied to the local data area of the submitted job.

7.4.4.2. Group Data Area

A group data area (an object of type *GDA) would be created by the operating system each time a group job is started. It is always of type *CHAR and its length is always 512 bytes long. This group data area cannot be deleted and lasts until the group job is ended. You can update and retrieve data from the group data area using CHGDTAARA, RTVDTAARA, and %SST as with the local data area.

7.4.4.3. PIP Data Area

A Program Initialization Parameter (PIP) data area is an object of type *PDA and is created by the operating system each time a prestart job is started. It is always 2000 characters long. As with the local data area and the group data area, you can retrieve and update data to the PDA using the CHGDTAARA, RTVDTAARA, and the %SST functions.

7.5. Using Messages

7.5.1. The Send Program Message Command

We use the SNDPGMMSG (Send Program Message) command to send messages to another program. These two programs can be in the same job or different jobs. There are two choices for the destination of the message to be sent. The message can be sent to the program message queue (object type *PGMQ) or a permanent message queue (object type *MSGQ). If both programs are on the same program stack, that is, if they are running in the same job, then you can send a message to both types of message queues, otherwise you have to send it to a permanent message queue only.

Figure 7.3 is the graphical representation of communication using messages.

Tip

A message queue is the place to receive messages. There are two types of message queues: permanent message queues, which are created by the CRTMSGQ command; and temporary message queues, which include program message queues.

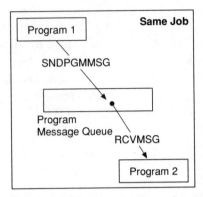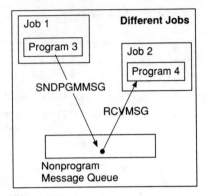

Figure 7.3. Communication using messages.

Some of the following will be covered in a later chapter where we will look into the details of the message handling commands.

The Send Program Message (SNDPGMMSG) command sends a program message to a named message queue, or to another program that has a RCVMSG (Receive Message) command. The message that the command sends can be an impromptu message or a predefined message. CL program variables can be embedded in the message text of a predefined message. The parameters of the SNDPGMMSG command include the following:

1. Message text (MSG)

   The message text is a string of characters of not more than 512 characters in length. If there are any special characters in the string, you need to enclose the string with quotes. This parameter is mutually exclusive with MSGID, MSGF, and MSGDTA since a message to be sent can either be impromptu or predefined. If you specified an impromptu message then all the parameters for a predefined message do not apply. Also, you cannot specify the message type as Escape, Notify, or Status because these message types would need the MSGID. In case you want to send the message to an external message queue of an interactive job then only the first 76 of the 512 characters of the message text will be displayed.

2. Message id (MSGID)

   The MSGID is the message identifier for any predefined message to be sent by the program. As mentioned above, if you have already specified the message text (MSG) you cannot enter MSGID, MSGF, and MSGDTA since you can only specify either an impromptu or predefined message. MSGID, MSGF, and MSGDTA parameters are only for predefined messages.

3. Message file (MSGF)

   The name of the message file that contains the MSGID of the predefined message to be sent. This parameter is required when you have specified the MSGID.

4. Message Data fields (MSGDTA)

   The message data fields are optional and contain the character string or CL character variables embedded in the predefined message. When the message is sent, the values of the variables are substituted in the message text as defined in the predefined message. The format of the data fields must be declared in the message description beforehand. If you send a message text (MSG), no message data fields are allowed. If you have more than one value to be embedded into the message text, you should first concatenate them to form one single character string.

5. The destination program Message Queue (TOPGMQ)

   This parameter specifies the program message queue to which the message is to be sent. The program message queue must be the message queue of a program called in the sending job. The name of the program message queue is always the same as the program name. Two values are to be entered to specify the program message queue. The first value is the relationship to the sending program; two values are possible for this parameter:

   *PRV — the message is going to be sent to the previous program

   *SAME — the message is going to be sent to the program message queue as specified in the second value below

   The second value is the program name. If you enter an * then the message will be sent to the program message queue of the sending program. Otherwise you have to enter the name of the program message queue. Besides the values mentioned above, you can also enter *EXT as the program message queue if the message is to be sent to the display station.

6. Permanent Message Queue (TOMSGQ)

   This parameter specifies any nonprogram message queue (i.e., permanent message queue) to which the message would be sent. You can specify the name of any message queue and the library that contains the message queue. Before you send the message to the specified message queue, make sure that you have the authority on that message queue otherwise the message will not be sent.

7. Destination User profile (TOUSR)

   This parameter specifies the user profile whose default message queue is used to receive the message you want to send. However, if you have already specified the program message queue or any permanent message queue, you cannot specify the receiving user profile.

8. Message Type (MSGTYP)

   This parameter specifies the type of message you want to send; for a more detailed explanation of the different message types see below.

9. Reply Message Queue (RPYMSGQ)

   This parameter specifies the program or nonprogram message queue to which the reply message for the inquiry or notify message will be sent.

10. CL variable for KEYVAR (KEYVAR)

    This parameter specifies the CL program variable that contains the message reference key that identified the message and is assigned by the system when the message is sent. This message reference key can be specified in the MSGKEY parameter of the RCVMSG command to receive the reply to an inquiry message being sent.

The SNDPGMMSG command is only valid in CL programs.
Sending program:

```
PGM
DCL VAR(&X) TYPE(*CHAR) LEN(10)
  .
  .
CHGVAR VAR(&X) VALUE('hello')
SNDPGMMSG MSGID(message id) MSGF(message file) +
  MSGDTA(&X) TOPGMQ(*SAME)
  .
  .
CALL PGM(receiving program name)
  .
```

```
.
ENDPGM
```

Receiving program:

```
PGM
DCL VAR(&A) TYPE(*CHAR) LEN(30)
.

.
.
RCVMSG PGMQ(*PRV) WAIT(0) MSG(&A)
.

.
.
ENDPGM
```

7.5.2. Message File and Message Descriptions

The sending and receiving programs in the previous section make use of the program message queue to send a predefined message from one program to another. In the example above, the predefined message is a message description stored in a message file and the message description is identified by the message identifier (MSGID).

You can use the Work Message File (WRKMSGF) command to create, maintain, or delete any predefined message. The message text of a predefined message can be changed at any time and after the message description is changed, you do not need to recompile any programs that use that message description.

For example, the message text of a predefined message has a variable embedded in it:

```
'I want to say &1'
```

The variable &1 is going to be substituted by a value supplied by the Send Program Message command at runtime. The attribute of variable &1 can be declared as *CHAR or *DEC.

The receiving program above receives the message from the program message queue. Please note that it specifies the program message queue as *PRV because this program is called by the program that sent the message. After the message is received, the message text is stored in a CL program variable named &A, which is declared as 30 characters. The value of variable &A is:

```
'I want to say hello '
```

which is a character string of length 30.

Remember that if you specify the program message queue as *EXT then the message is sent to the display station and the

RCVMSG command in the receiving program is not able to capture its value and return it to a variable.

The same thing is true for *PRV. If you specify the program message queue as *PRV, the message is sent to the system Command Entry panel, because that is the place the program was called. Actually the Command Entry panel is invoked by a system program called QCMD, as already mentioned in Chapter 2.

You can also explicitly specify the program message queue name as follows:

Sending program:

```
SNDPGMMSG MSGID(message id) MSGF(message file) +
   MSGDTA(&X) +
   TOPGMQ(*SAME program-message-queue)
```

Receiving program:

```
RCVMSG PGMQ(*SAME program-message-queue) +
   WAIT(0) MSG(&A)
```

If you are sending the message to a permanent message queue:
Sending program:

```
SNDPGMMSG MSGID(message id) MSGF(message file) +
   MSGDTA(&X) +
   TOMSGQ(library name/message queue)
```

Receiving program:

```
RCVMSG MSGQ(library name/message queue) +
   WAIT(0) MSG(&A)
```

Tip

A message file is the place to store message descriptions; message descriptions are the definitions of the predefined messages.

7.5.3. How to Receive Messages

We use the Receive Message (RCVMSG) command to receive messages that are sent from a Send Program Message command. This command copies the message received in the specified message queue and returns its value to CL program variables in the program. You can specify the message type, the reference key, or both when you want to selectively receive a message from the message queue. You can also specify whether the message received would be removed or left in the message queue after it is received.

We will receive all the messages from message queues. A message queue is an object on the system that can be shared among several users. You can always clear all the messages from a message queue using the Clear Message Queue (CLRMSGQ) command. To avoid the message queue being cleared by other users before your receiving program is run, you should always allocate the message queue with the ALCOBJ command in your program. It is very important to allocate the message queue before the program is run since the RCVMSG command will only allocate the message queue implicitly when the command is run.

You can also specify the waiting time for incoming messages in the RCVMSG command.

The parameters of the RCVMSG command include:

1. Program message queue (PGMQ)

   It specifies the program message queue from which the program receives the message. The values allowed in this parameter are the same as those in the SNDPGMMSG command.

2. Message Queue (MSGQ)

   This parameter specifies the nonprogram message queue where the message was put.

3. Message Type (MSGTYPE)

4. Message Key (MSGKEY)

   It is the reference key of the message received. Values allowed include:

   *NONE—When no reference key is specified.

   *TOP—It causes the first message on the message queue to be received and it can be used only when the message type is *NEXT. Besides these two predefined values, you can also enter the CL variable that contains the reference key.

5. Wait time (WAIT)

   It specifies the length of time in seconds the receiving program will wait for the message to arrive at the message queue. If there isn't any message on the queue at the time the RCVMSG command is executed, the program will wait for the amount of time specified in this parameter.

6. Remove message (RMV)

   It specifies whether the message received is removed from the message queue after it is received or kept in the mes-

sage queue as an old message. You can specify the CL variables to return the values of the message received in the
RCVMSG command.

7.5.4. Types of Messages

The types of messages (MSGTYP) that you can send using the
SNDPGMMSG command include the following:

1. Informational
2. Inquiry
3. Request
4. Completion
5. Diagnostic
6. Notify
7. Escape
8. Status

Each of these will be explained in more detail in the chapter on
message handling.

You can send all types of messages except escape messages to
an external message queue, and all types of messages except inquiry
messages to any program message queue. You can receive messages
by message type, by reference key, or by a combination of both.

```
RCVMSG MSGQ(message-queue) MSGTYP(*INQ) +
   MSG(&A)
```

The statement above receives messages by message type. The
message queue contains different types of messages; you can always
specify what type you want to receive in the RCVMSG command.
The statement above receives inquiry messages only from the message queue named in the First-In-First-Out (FIFO) manner.

7.6. Using a Data Queue

7.6.1. What Is a Data Queue?

A data queue is an object of type *DTAQ. A data queue is a place to
store data; its organization is like a message queue or job queue. One
characteristic of a data queue is that each record in the queue can be
retrieved by a pending program, and once that record has been received it is removed from the data queue. On the other hand, records
read from a database file will still physically be on that file unless

the program deletes them. That is the main difference between data queue and database files.

Figure 7.4 illustrates how a data queue works.

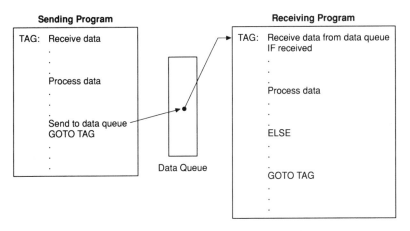

Figure 7.4. How a data queue works.

By using a data queue, we can break down a single-thread job into multithread jobs, each having different functionality. We can separate the interactive part, which requires user interactions, from the batch processing part, which does not require any user intervention at all. For example, we can separate the data entry part and the master file update part.

The scenario is this: we have one interactive program handling data entry and validations, and as soon as the data has been entered it is sent to a data queue. We have a batch program running all day long that picks up the data from the data queue for master file updates. This separation of functionality does improve the overall performance because this approach now relieves the QINTER subsystem from heavy file I/O. See Figure 7.5 for an illustration.

A data queue is the fastest in asynchronous communication and it has less overhead than a database file. For example, to add a record to a database file, the system needs to update the index files as well, thus incurring higher overhead. A data queue would not have this problem.

In addition, more than one job can receive data from the same data queue, and any number of jobs can send data to the same data

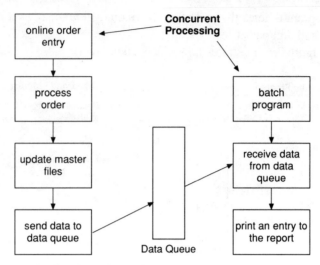

Figure 7.5. Application using a data queue.

queue, so a data queue is very good for concurrent processing. But although more than one job can receive data from a data queue, only one program will be able to receive one particular entry from the data queue while the other jobs are waiting. Once an entry in the queue is received by a program, it is removed from the data queue.

However, we should bear in mind that a data queue is not for long-term storage of data. Also, when the entries of a data queue grow larger and larger, system performance is degraded.

7.6.2. How to Create a Data Queue

Data queues are created using the Create Data Queue (CRTDTAQ) command. Parameters for this command include:

1. Data queue name
2. Maximum entry length
3. Sequence
4. Text description
5. Force to auxiliary storage
6. Include sender ID
7. Authority

We can specify the maximum length for an entry in the range of 1 to 64,512 bytes.

The parameter "Sequence" specifies the processing sequence of the data queue. Entries on a data queue could be handled in the following ways:

1. First-In-First-Out (FIFO)
2. Last-In-First-Out (LIFO)
3. Keyed

If you want the data queue to be keyed, you need to specify the key length in the CRTDTAQ command as well.

There is another parameter called "Force to auxiliary storage" and it indicates whether you want to write to the DASD storage whenever an entry arrives or leaves the data queue.

7.6.3. Other Commands Related to Data Queue

Data queues can be deleted using the Delete Data Queue (DLTDTAQ) command as shown:

```
DLTDTAQ DTAQ(data-queue-name)
```

There is no OS/400 command that can display the contents of a data queue like that for a data area or physical file. If you want to do this, you need to write some programs to accomplish this purpose. You can find the source codes for the display data queue function in the IBM-provided library named QUSRTOOL. Figure 7.6 shows you the contents of a data queue by running this small utility program.

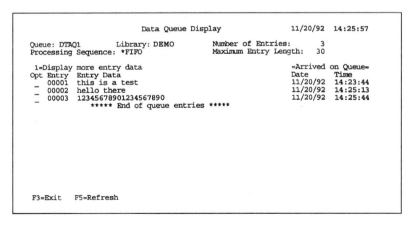

Figure 7.6. Data Queue display.

7.6.4. How to Send and Receive Data with a Data Queue

There are no OS/400 commands to send and receive data to and from a data queue, but instead there are two system programs provided by IBM that we can call in our CL program to accomplish this task.

The program that we can call in our CL program to send data to a data queue is called QSNDDTAQ. You can use the program in the following syntax:

```
CALL PGM(QSNDDTAQ) PARM(&1 &2 &3 &4)
```

where &1, &2, &3, and &4 are the parameters of the program:

&1 — data queue name that is declared as character variable of length 10.

&2 — library name that contains the data queue; it should be declared as character variable of length 10. Predefined value *LIBL can be used.

&3 — the number of bytes of data to be sent to the data queue; it should be declared as decimal variable of length 5 and no decimal point.

&4 — the variable that contains the data to be sent to the data queue; it should be declared as a character variable.

In your CL program, you may specify this variable as a decimal variable and the QSNDDTAQ program would still run, but you will not get the correct data sent to the queue and unexpected results may occur.

If the length of data (&4) sent to the data queue is greater than the length specified in variable &3 in the QSNDDTAQ function, the characters exceeding the length specified would be truncated.

If the length of data sent to the data queue is greater than the maximum length parameter specified when you create the data queue, then an error will occur and data will not be sent. For example, if 32 bytes of data are sent to the data queue but the data queue's maximum length is only 30 bytes, then the data will not be sent.

The program that receives data from a data queue is called a server program or server job. As already mentioned above, there is no OS/400 command to retrieve data from a data queue and we have to use a system-supplied program named QRCVDTAQ to receive data in our server program. You can incorporate the following function in your CL program to receive data from a data queue:

```
CALL PGM(QRCVDTAQ) PARM(&QNAME &LIBNAME + &LEN &DATA
            &WAIT)
```

The syntax of the call command would be:

```
CALL PGM(QRCVDTAQ) PARM(&1 &2 &3 &4 &5)
```

where &1, &2, &3, &4, and &5 are the parameters of the program:

&1 — data queue name that is declared as character variable of length 10.

&2 — library name that contains the data queue; it should be declared as character variable of length 10. Predefined value *LIBL can be used.

&3 — the number of bytes of data to be received from the data queue; it should be declared as decimal variable of length 5 and no decimal point.

&4 — the variable that will contain the data to be received from the data queue; it should be declared as a character variable.

&5 — it is the wait time; it should be declared as a decimal variable.

If you specify a 0 as the wait time, the program will return immediately, no matter if data has been received or not.

If you specify a positive integer, it represents the number of seconds the program would wait until it returns if no data has been received.

If you specify a negative integer, the program will wait indefinitely until a record is received from the data queue.

Once an entry in the data queue is received, it will be removed from the data queue. Therefore we have a potential problem for losing data if the receiving program ends abnormally before the record received from the data queue is processed. That record will be lost and there is no way to retrieve it. We may want to implement some abnormal end handling procedure in the program to handle this situation.

As mentioned above, more than one program can be waiting for entries from a data queue but only one program will receive one particular entry from the queue. Which program would receive an entry first is mainly determined by the job priority.

There is no AS/400 command to clear a data queue but there is a system-supplied program that achieves the same purpose; the program is named QCLRDTAQ. The following statement illustrates how this is done in our CL programs:

```
CALL PGM(QCLRDTAQ) PARM(&QNAME &LIBNAME)
```

This function needs two parameters:

&QNAME — it is the name of the data queue and is a character variable of length 10.

&LIBNAME — it is the name of the library that contains the data queue and it is a character variable of length 10.

One thing to bear in mind is that the auxiliary storage allocated to a data queue will not be freed after an entry is received by a program; the size of a data queue will grow larger and larger. Therefore it is necessary to delete and re-create the data queue periodically. We should implement this when we design our application.

7.7. Using Switches

For each job running on the AS/400 system, whether or not it is interactive or a batch job, there are eight switches associated with each job. The value for each switch is either a 0 or 1 to represent the ON or OFF position. The switches exist on an AS/400 mainly for compatibility reasons (since System/3 actually has eight switches that could be manually set by the operator).

You can find out the switch setting for your current job by using the following command:

```
DSPJOB
```

Choose option 2 from the Display Job menu to display the job status definition attributes. On the second screen of the job definition attributes display you will see the switch setting.

When the current job is started on the system, the switch setting of the job description of the user profile is fetched and copied into the switch setting of the current job; this remains unchanged until they are altered by the user. You can change the switch setting for your current job by using the CHGJOB command; the following statement changes the switch setting to 11110000:

```
CHGJOB SWS(11110000)
```

When a new job is started, it takes the switch setting as specified in the job description (*JOBD). If it is a batch job submitted by the Submit Job (SBMJOB) command you can specify the new switch setting of the batch job explicitly at the SWITCH parameter:

```
SBMJOB CMD(CALL PGM(program)) SWS(11110000)
```

You can test the switch setting by using the %SWITCH function in the CL program. The syntax of the Switch function is:

```
%SWITCH(8-character-mask)
```

The 8-character-mask indicates which switch will be compared and what values they are compared with. Each position in the 8-character-mask can be:

0 — off
1 — on
X — ignored

For example, %SWITCH(1100X01X) is going to compare the switches for the job and see if:

first switch is on and
second switch is on and
third switch is off and
fourth switch is off and
sixth switch is off and
seventh switch is on

and if the IF statement is evaluated as true, it will return a value of 1, otherwise it returns 0.

In the CL programs you can combine the IF statement, the SBMJOB command, and the CHGJOB command to control the flow of the program. Figure 7.7 shows you how to pass the switches from one program to another.

The disadvantage of using the switch is that the amount of information to pass from program to program would be very limited.

7.8. Comparing the Different Modes of Communication

The table in Figure 7.8 compares the different modes of communication between programs. The first column compares their storage methods, and the second column compares the requirements of the sender and receiver programs.

```
PGM
DCL          VAR(&A) TYPE(*DEC) LEN(3 0)
DCL          VAR(&SWITCH) TYPE(*CHAR) LEN(8)
.
.
.
IF           COND(&A > 0) THEN(CHGJOB SWS(10000000))
ELSE         CMD(CHGJOB SWS(01000000))
.
.
.
RTVJOBA      SWS(&SWITCH)
SBMJOB       CMD(CALL PGM(PGM1)) SWS(&SWITCH)
.
.
.
ENDPGM
```

Figure 7.7. Using job switches to pass information.

Parameters	—Stored in main memory	Sender and receiver programs must be on the same program stack.
Data Area	—Local data area stored in main memory —Permanent data area stored on disk	Receiver program must be submitted by the sender program if using local data area; otherwise they do not need to be in the same job.
Messages	—Some stored in main memory, some stored on disk; depends on the type of message queue	Receiver program and sender program must be in the same job if using program message queue; otherwise they do not need to be in the same job.
Data Queue	—Stored on disk	Sender and receiver do not need to be in the same job.
Switches	—Stored in main memory	Sender and receiver programs need to be in the same job.

Figure 7.8. Comparing different modes of communication.

Command Summary

CRTDTAARA   Create a Data Area

DLTDTAARA   Delete a Data Area

CHGDTAARA   Change a Data Area

RTVDTAARA   Retrieve from a Data Area

SNDPGMMSG   Send Program Message

RCVMSG   Receive Message

Exercises

7.1. Explain how to pass the following from one CL program to another as a parameter:
- Program variables, numeric and character
- Numeric constant
- Character constant

7.2. What commands are used to update a data area? Retrieve from a data area?

7.3. What are the characteristics of a local data area?

7.4. What commands are used to send messages to another program? Retrieve messages from another program?

7.5. What functions are used to send data to a data queue? Receive data from a data queue?

Message Handling

This chapter introduces the message-handling mechanism on the AS/400 and the set of message-handling commands.

As we have learned in the previous chapter, a message can be used to pass information between programs. A message is also a way of communicating from:

- user to user
- user to program
- program to program

When a user issues a system command, he is actually sending a request message (message type *RQS) to the current job and requesting that a particular task be done.

There are several other types of messages on the AS/400 serving various purposes, for example, program messages (sent by SNDPGMMSG command) that are employed by one program to pass information to another program.

We will examine the different types of messages and the mechanism of message handling in more detail in this chapter.

8.1. Categories of Messages

We can broadly classify messages into three basic categories by their origins.

8.1.1. Impromptu Messages

They are composed by the user on the fly; most of the time these impromptu messages are used for one-time-only messages, for example, "Did you read the news about the new AS/400 F-series models?"

8.1.2. Program-described Messages

They are hardcoded into programs and compiled into executable files; they are sent to any message queue by calling the program.

8.1.3. Predefined Messages

These messages, including the message contents and message attributes, are stored in the message file (object type is *MSGF). You can substitute the variables in the message text with the message data when the message is sent. They are identified by the message identifier number. They can be reused as many times as needed.

Tip

No matter whether it is an impromptu message, a program-described message, or a predefined message, the message must have a message text and the message parameters associated with it and must be sent by a message-sending command.

When a specific situation occurs more than once in the application and the message can be reused in more than one program, we can make use of predefined messages. Such messages are defined by their message descriptions and stored in a message file.

For example, we may want to send a message to a user asking for the number of copies he wants in the report printing programs, or we may want to send a completion message saying "the batch job is completed normally" by the end of the batch processing programs. In these cases we can define them beforehand as message descriptions in a message file since such messages are universal to all similar programs. By making use of message descriptions and a message file we can achieve software reusability.

Another advantage of using a message file and predefined messages is that only messages in a message file can accept message data.

8.2. Message Queue

No matter whether the message you send is an impromptu message, a program-described message, or a predefined message, the message has to be delivered to a message queue.

8.2.1. What Is a Message Queue?

A message queue is an object of object type *MSGQ. It is the place to store the messages sent from a message sender. The way it stores messages is just like other queue objects, such as job queue and output queue. Messages are accumulated one after another in their arrival sequence in the message queue. However, the way the messages are handled and processed can differ. They can be retrieved in the First-In-First-Out manner, First-In-Last-Out manner, by message key, by message type, or by the combination of message key and message type from the message queue.

8.2.2. Types of Message Queues

There are two main types of message queues:

- Permanent message queue
- Temporary message queue

8.2.2.1. Permanent Message Queue

Permanent message queues are objects of type *MSGQ and are stored in libraries. They can exist independent of any user, program, or file.

You can create permanent message queues by the Create Message Queue (CRTMSGQ) command:

```
CRTMSGQ MSGQ(library/message-queue-name) +
    SIZE(*NOMAX) AUT(*CHANGE)
```

This command creates a user-defined message queue and stores it in the library specified. One thing we need to pay attention to is the authority to the library that contains the message queue. The authority to the library for the public should be set to *USE so that other users and jobs can send messages to this message queue. Without the proper authority set, the user or job receives an error message when they send the message to the message queue. You can also set the following additional requirements in the parameters of the CRTMSGQ command:

1. Force to auxiliary storage

    This parameter specifies whether any messages added to or removed from the message queue, or any changes made to the message queue descriptions, will be updated to auxiliary storage immediately. It is a safety measure: in case a power failure happens, any messages added to or removed from the message queue, or any changes made to the message queue descriptions, will not be lost.

2. Queue size

    You can specify the initial size of the message queue, the increment values, and the number of increments allowed. If you are not sure about the expected receiving volume of the message queue, it is better to specify *NOMAX in the size parameter.

3. Authority

    You can specify the authority to the message queue for the users who do not have any specific authority to the message queue. The authority that you can specify includes *CHANGE, *USE, *ALL, and *EXCLUDE. You need to specify at least the *USE authority to the public for them to send messages to the queue and read messages from it.

Besides the ones created by the CRTMSGQ command, there are some other permanent message queues created automatically by the system. These are the message queues associated with user profile and device description.

Whenever a user profile or device description is created, a message queue is automatically created by the system for that user profile or device description with the same name. Therefore, if a new user JOHN is added to the system, a new message queue named JOHN is created by the system as well. If a device description DSP50 is created, a message queue named DSP50 is created automatically.

There is another kind of permanent message queue besides the ones mentioned above. This message queue is the System Operator's Message Queue (QSYSOPR) which is shipped by IBM when you purchase the machine.

As mentioned above, message queues are automatically created when user profile or device descriptions are created, however, for certain devices like tape drives, printers, or communication devices, we have the option of a new message queue for the device or the default message queue. If we do not specify any new message queue when we create the device descriptions, the system uses QSYSOPR as the default message queue.

One thing to bear in mind is that when the QSYSOPR message queue is set at *BREAK mode and the system operator fails to respond to the message, all subsequent messages fail to break until the first one is responded to. The other messages break when the first message gets the reply and the message queue is freed up again. If you do not want this to happen, set the QSYSOPR message queue to *NOTIFY mode, or put a break-handling program on the message queue.

Tip

Permanent message queues include message queues created by the CRTMSGQ command, message queues associated with user profile and device descriptions, and system operator message queues.

8.2.2.2. Temporary Message Queue

There are two types of temporary message queues:

- External message queues (*EXT)
- Program message queues (*PGMQ)

Exactly one external message queue is created for each job active on the system. For an interactive job, the external message queue is the display station of the requester, therefore, every time you enter a command at the command line, you are actually sending one request message to the external message queue of the current job. Your request message is received from the external message queue and the operating system interprets and processes it. If the job needs to report any abnormal situations to you, it sends the message to the external message queue as well.

For a batch job, the system uses the QSYSOPR message queue as the external message queue. An external message queue for an interactive job only exists for the lifetime of the active job. Once you sign off, the external message queue of the job vanishes.

For each program on the program stack, the system creates a temporary message queue for that program. The name of the program message queue is the same as the program. If the program is called more than once from different programs, there are program message queues with the same names. The program message queue can be used to pass information between programs.

If you send an Informational or diagnostic message to the external message queue, the message appears in the Program Message panel and the program stops running until you press <ENTER>. On the other hand, a status message does not prevent the program from running.

We can always determine the destination of the message that we want to send in our CL programs by specifying either the MSGQ or the PGMQ parameters in the send message commands. However, these two parameters are mutually exclusive.

The parameter MSGQ, when specified, indicates that a permanent message queue is used while PGMQ, when specified, always indicates that a temporary message queue is used.

Tip

Specify a permanent message queue at the MSGQ parameter; on the other hand, specify a temporary message queue at the PGMQ parameter.

8.2.3. How to Display Messages

Messages can be displayed by the Display Message (DSPMSG) command. You can choose the message queue by specifying the message queue parameter in the display message command. You can also filter the messages by specifying the message types and/or severity code. The DSPMSG command can display messages stored in user profile message queues, device message queues, and system operator message queues. For example, you can display messages in the system operator's message queue as follows:

```
DSPMSG QSYSOPR
```

Usually you may see several notify and inquiry messages waiting for reply in the QSYSOPR message queue. The author recommends against responses to any particular IBM-provided system operator message, even one as relatively harmless as this one.

8.2.4. Other Commands Related to Message Queue

The Change Message Queue (CHGMSGQ) command can change the attributes of the specified message queue. The specified message queue can be a permanent message queue or a temporary message queue for the workstation or user profile. When you want to run this command, make sure you have at least the *CHANGE authority to the message queue object.

Message queue attributes that you can change include:

1. Delivery mode
   This parameter specifies how messages are to be sent to the message queue. The predefined value *HOLD indicates that the messages are held in the message queue until the Display Message (DSPMSG) command is run on the message queue or the Receive message (RCVMSG) command is run on the message queue in a CL program. When you change the delivery mode to either the *BREAK or *NOTIFY mode, the message queue is allocated by the current job, and from now on the current job is interrupted whenever a message is sent to the specified message queue. If the message queue is already allocated by another job, the CHGMSGQ command is not processed. If you change the delivery mode to *DFT mode, any inquiry message sent to the message queue is replied to automatically by the system with the default reply; on the other hand, if the message sent is just an informational message, the message is ignored.

2. Severity code filter
   The severity level specified in this parameter serves as a filter of messages. Any messages with severity level equal to or greater than the specified severity level are sent to the message queue in the *BREAK or *NOTIFY mode. Any other messages with severity levels lower than the specified severity level are kept in the message queue until the DSPMSG command or the RCVMSG command is run.

3. Break handling program
   This parameter specifies the program to be called when any break message is sent to the message queue.

4. Reset old messages
   As we can remember, data records on a data queue are removed once it is received by a program; however, messages can still remain in the message queue once they are dis-

played or received. Messages that have already been received or displayed would be marked as old messages internally by the system. Any messages that arrive after the DSPMSG or RCVMSG command was run are marked as new messages. However, the CHGMSGQ command allows you to reset the message flag from old to new if you specify the *YES value at the RESET parameter.

Messages stored in a message queue can be cleared by the Clear Message Queue (CLRMSGQ) command. This command removes all messages from the message queue:

```
CLRMSGQ MSGQ(library-name/message-queue-name)
```

Sometimes you may want to clear the message queue before your program starts to receive any messages from the message queue. This makes sure that your program does not receive any out-of-date messages that you do not want. You can implement the CLRMSGQ command in your CL program.

8.3. Message File and Message Descriptions

8.3.1. How to Create a Message File

Predefined messages have to be stored in a message file. Message files are objects of type *MSGF where message descriptions are stored. You can create a message file by the Create Message File (CRTMSGF) command:

```
CRTMSGF MSGF(library name/message file name)
```

A message file is a place to store message descriptions. Each message description is one predefined message. Similar to a message queue, we need to pay attention to the authority of the message file. If the user has no authority to a message file, then the user would not be able to retrieve any message description from the message file and send the message as required. Therefore, we need to impose at least the *USE authority to the message file so that the other users can send messages contained in the message file as well.

There are some special parameters you can specify when you create the message file:

1. Message file size
   It is important to calculate the size needed for your message file when you create it, since once it is created and becomes full, you will not be able to change the size of the message

file. Therefore, use the size parameter to specify the initial storage size of the message file. The minimum size of a message file is 1KB and the maximum is 16,000 KB. You can specify the initial size of the message file, the size of each increment, and the number of increments allowed. These amounts are all expressed in kilobytes. If you are not sure about the expected size of the message file, you should specify *NOMAX as the file size. It allows you to add message descriptions until the message file cannot hold them any more; this maximum size is determined by the system.

2. Authority

This specifies the level of authority granted to users who have no specific authority to the message file. You can specify *CHANGE, *USE, *ALL, and *EXCLUDE. But if you want the ordinary users be able to use the message descriptions in your message file, you should grant them at least the *USE authority to the message file.

When you name message files, do not start their names with the letter Q since the system message files on the AS/400 system such as QCPFMSG and QRPGMSG are started with the letter Q. System message files store system error messages.

8.3.2. Message Descriptions

Message descriptions are the definitions of the message.

When you want to create a new message, you need to add a message description to the message file. The number of message descriptions that you can add to a message file is determined by the size parameter in the CRTMSGF command. Each message description is identified by a unique message identification number that is 7 characters long and in the following format:

    pppnnnn

where the first three characters must be one alphabetic followed by two alphamerics, and the last 4 characters can be any decimals or characters. You should avoid using ADM, CPA, CPC, CPD, CPF, CPI, MCH, or RPG for the first three characters since the IBM-supplied system messages also begin with these characters. For example, the system messages in system message file QCPFMSG are all identified by CPFXXXX.

The command that you use to add a message description to a message file is the Add Message Description (ADDMSGD) command.

Figures 8.1(a) and (b) are the Add Message Description (ADDMSGD) screens.

```
                        Add Message Description (ADDMSGD)

      Type choices, press Enter

      Message identifier . . . . . . .   msg0001      Name
      Message file . . . . . . . . . .   msgf         Name
        Library. . . . . . . . . . .     *LIBL        Name, *LIBL, *CURLIB
      First-level message text . . . .   File &1 cannot be found.


      Second-level message text. . . .   *NONE




      Severity code. . . . . . . . . .   00           0-99             . . .

                                                                    More...
      F3=Exit    F4=Prompt   F5=Refresh  F10=Additional parameters  F12=Cancel
      F13=How to use this display       F24=More keys
```

Figure 8.1(a).

```
                        Add Message Description (ADDMSGD)

      Type choices, press Enter

      Message data fields formats:
        Data type  . . . . . . . . . .   *char        *NONE, *QTDCHAR, *CHAR...
        Length . . . . . . . . . . .     10           Number, *VARY
        *VARY bytes or dec pos . . . .                Number
                + for more values
      Reply type . . . . . . . . . . .   *CHAR        *CHAR, *DEC, *ALPHA, *NAME...
      Maximum reply lengths: . . . . .
        Length . . . . . . . . . . . .   *TYPE        Number, *TYPE, *NONE
        Decimal positions  . . . . . .                Number
      Valid reply values . . . . . . .   *NONE
                + for more values
      Special reply values:
        Original from-value  . . . . .   *NONE
        Replacement to-value . . . . .
                + for more values
                                                                    More...
      F3=Exit    F4=Prompt   F5=Refresh  F10=Additional parameters  F12=Cancel
      F13=How to use this display       F24=More keys
```

Figure 8.1(b).

You can see that the first-level message text is "File &1 cannot be found.", where &1 is a substitute variable embedded in the message text. The value of the substitute variable is determined in the send message command. You should also specify the data type for the embedded variable when you define the message descriptions. In our example, the embedded variable in the message text is a character variable of length 10.

As you see in the figures, the ADDMSGD command adds a message description with identification number MSG0001 to the message file. The message text of the message reads "File &1 cannot be found." and its severity code is 00.

The type of message and the delivery mode are not defined in the message description in advance; instead, they will be determined in the send message command.

The special requirements that you can specify while creating your message description include the following:

1. First-level message text (MSG)

   This is the first-level message text that is to be sent to a message queue. The maximum length of the first-level message text is 132 bytes long. You can embed substitution variables in the message text to indicate any fields to be replaced in the message by the program. The substitution variables always begin with ampersand (&) followed by a digit. For example, the message text can read:

   ```
   There are &1 records processed; &2 successes and &3
   failures.
   ```

   The program replaces &1, &2, and &3 by the three variables or constants specified in the Send Program Message (SNDPGMMSG) command before the actual message is being sent. So defining message descriptions with substitution variables allows more flexibility and reusability.

2. Second-level message text (SECLVL)

   The second-level message text is to supply additional information to the user upon pressing the <HELP> key; it acts as an extension to the first-level message text. The maximum length of the second-level message text is 3000 bytes. Like the first-level message text, you can embed substitution variables in the second-level message text and the program replaces them with values specified in the Send Message command that actually sends the message.

3. Severity level (SEV)

The severity code of a message describes the level of severity that is associated with a message and also indicates the minimum condition that causes the message to be sent. In the case of running a batch job, the severity level can cause the batch job to end. In the case of an interactive job, the severity level can cause the processing of the command to be aborted. The severity code is a 2-digit value that ranges from 00 to 99. The higher the value the more severe is the condition. If the severity level is not specified for the message, the message assumes that the severity level is 00. Usually the severity code for the message should correspond to the severity code predefined by IBM. However, you can assign any 2-digit value to the severity code even if no such severity code has been predefined by IBM. The predefined values of the severity codes and their meanings are as follows:

00 — Informational
10 — Warning
20 — Error
30 — Severe Error
40 — Abnormal End of Program or Function
50 — Abnormal End of Job
60 — System Status
70 — Device Integrity
80 — System Alert
90 — System Integrity
99 — Action

4. Format of the message data fields (FMT)

This is needed when embedded substitution variables appear in the first- and second-level message texts. The format of the message data fields are the data types of the substitution variables embedded in these texts. When you send the message by the Send Program Message (SNDPGMMSG) command, you need to specify the program variables whose values are to be substituted into the message, and their data types must match those defined in the message descriptions.

The following parameters are specified relating to the reply that is expected if the message is sent as an inquiry message that needs a reply. These parameters are used to describe the reply message. These parameters are not compulsory for a message to allow a reply, but they can be used to define valid replies to the message.

5. Type of reply (Type)

   This parameter specifies the type of replies that are valid replies to the message that is sent as an inquiry or notify message. The predefined values that are valid for this parameter include: *CHAR, *DEC, *ALPHA, *NAME, and *NONE.

6. The maximum length of the reply (LEN)

   This parameter specifies the maximum length of the reply if the message is sent as an inquiry or notify message. The parameter takes predefined values *TYPE and *NONE, or any length that is allowed by the system. If you specify *TYPE as the maximum length of the parameter, the program checks the data type of the reply and determines its maximum length allowed. Therefore, if the data type is *CHAR, the maximum length allowed is 132 bytes long; if the data type is *DEC, the maximum length of the reply is 15 digits, in which 9 digits are after the decimal point. If the data type is *NAME, the maximum length allowed is 10 characters.

7. List of valid replies (VALUES)

   This parameter lets you specify a list of values that are valid replies to the message sent, if the message is sent as an inquiry or notify message. You can specify up to 20 values in the list and each of them must comply with the requirements as set down in the TYPE and LEN parameters. If such a list is specified in the ADDMSGD command, the reply to the message must match one of the values in the list, if the message is sent as an inquiry or notify message.

8. Special Values (SPCVAL)

   You can specify 1 to 20 sets of from-value and to-value to determine the reply sent to the sender of the message. The from-value in each set is compared with the reply, and an optional to-value is sent as the reply if its corresponding from-value matches the reply. Of course, the message must be sent as an inquiry or notify message for the special values to be applicable.

9. Upper and lower limits for valid replies (RANGE)

   These parameters specify the upper and lower limits for the values of a valid reply to the message if it is sent as an inquiry or notify message. These values must comply with the TYPE and LEN parameters as specified earlier.

10. Relation that must be met for valid replies (REL)

This parameter specifies the relation that must be met by the reply for it to be valid for the message, if it is sent as an inquiry or notify message. You have to specify the operator and a value. Valid operators include *LT, *LE, *GT, *GE, *NL (not less than), *NG (not greater than), *NE, and *EQ. The value specified in the relation must comply with the *TYPE and *LEN parameters.

One thing you need to bear in mind is that if you have specified the VALUES parameter, you cannot specify the RANGE and REL parameters.

Sometimes you may encounter an error message sent by the system when you are running your application program. You can use the Display Message Descriptions (DSPMSGD) command to display the message text and details of these messages:

```
DSPMSGD CPF9801
```

8.4. How to Send a Message

After the message description is defined, we can use it to send a message to a message queue in your CL program.

The delivery mode of the message (that is, should the message be sent as a break message or just an informational message) is determined by the *MSGTYP parameter in the send message command. The mode of delivery is not defined in the message description in advance. Also the destination of the message is determined in the message sending command as well.

The SNDPGMMSG statement that follows shows that an escape message was sent to a program message queue:

```
SNDPGMMSG MSGID(.....) MSGF(.....) TOPGMQ(*SAME) +
   MSGTYPE(*ESCAPE)
```

The following statement shows that an escape message was sent to a permanent message queue (the QSYSOPR message queue):

```
SNDPGMMSG MSGID(.....) MSGF(.....) TOMSGQ(QSYSOPR) +
   MSGTYPE(*ESCAPE)
```

The following statement shows that the escape message was sent to a message queue associated with a user profile:

```
SNDPGMMSG MSGID(.....) MSGF(.....) TOUSR(user-profile) +
   MSGTYPE(*ESCAPE)
```

The delivery of the message would involve a send message command.

8.4.1. Commands That Send a Message

On the AS/400, there are quite a few send message commands that you can choose. These include:

8.4.1.1. Send Message (SNDMSG)

The Send Message (SNDMSG) command is used by the workstation user to send an impromptu message to a message queue. You cannot send a message defined in a message file with this command. The message sender can require a reply from the receiver of the message as well, if the message is sent as an inquiry or notify message. The message text can have a maximum length of 512 bytes, and you need to specify the destination of the message, be it a user profile or a message queue. The message types allowed in this command are *INFO and *INQ only. The inquiry message is sent to only one message queue at a time and the message requires a reply. If no reply is entered by the receiver, the system replies with the default reply value.

8.4.1.2. Send Program Message (SNDPGMMSG)

The Send Program Message (SNDPGMMSG) command is used by a program to send a program message to a named message queue, or to another program that has the Receive Message (RCVMSG) command implemented in it. The SNDPGMMSG command is the most often used command to send a message in CL programmings because it can send both impromptu messages and predefined messages to any type of message queue. This command is only valid in CL programs. We will discuss this command later.

8.4.1.3. Send User Message (SNDUSRMSG)

The Send User Message (SNDUSRMSG) command is used by a program to send a message to a message queue and, optionally, receive a reply for that message. You can send either an impromptu message or a predefined message using this command and, like the SNDPGMMSG command, it is only valid in CL programs. This command is actually a hybrid of the SNDPGMMSG and RCVMSG commands because it uses a combination of parameters available to the SNDPGMMSG and RCVMSG commands so that we can send and receive messages from a program in one single command. You can specify any impromptu or predefined message to be sent and define the substitution variables in the message data parameters in the command. The message types that are allowed are *INFO and *INQ messages. You can send the message either to a user profile or to a message queue. In the same command, you can specify the CL variable to contain the reply to the message, and you can define the CL variable as a character field with length up to 132 bytes. This parameter is applicable only when the message type is *INQ. If the reply is longer than defined, it would be truncated.

8.4.1.4. Send Break Message (SNDBRKMSG)

The Send Break Message (SNDBRKMSG) command is used to send an impromptu message to one or more display station message queues. The command causes the message to be sent in break mode; however, not all of the receivers receive the message in the break mode because it all depends on the value of the BRKMSG attribute in the user's job description. This command is coded into CL program and run by batch when it is necessary to prompt the receiver for some vital information for the program. You can specify a message text of length not longer than 512 bytes. You need to specify the message queue where the message is going to be sent. The message types that you can specify are *INFO and *INQ messages.

8.4.1.5. Send Network Message (SNDNETMSG)

In summary, the SNDMSG and SNDBRKMSG commands are intended primarily to be used to send messages interactively by workstation users. On the other hand, the SNDPGMMSG and SNDUSRMSG commands are used predominantly in CL programs for sending program messages to different kinds of message queues.

The program in Figure 8.2 is an example of using the SNDPGMMSG and RCVMSG commands for sending messages to the current job's program message queue and receiving the message from the job's message queue into the program.

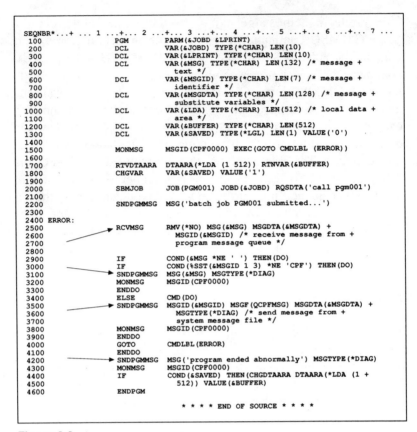

```
SEQNBR*...+ ... 1 ...+... 2 ...+... 3 ...+... 4 ...+... 5 ...+... 6 ...+... 7 ...
   100          PGM        PARM(&JOBD &LPRINT)
   200          DCL        VAR(&JOBD) TYPE(*CHAR) LEN(10)
   300          DCL        VAR(&LPRINT) TYPE(*CHAR) LEN(10)
   400          DCL        VAR(&MSG) TYPE(*CHAR) LEN(132) /* message +
   500                       text */
   600          DCL        VAR(&MSGID) TYPE(*CHAR) LEN(7) /* message +
   700                       identifier */
   800          DCL        VAR(&MSGDTA) TYPE(*CHAR) LEN(128) /* message +
   900                       substitute variables */
  1000          DCL        VAR(&LDA) TYPE(*CHAR) LEN(512) /* local data +
  1100                       area */
  1200          DCL        VAR(&BUFFER) TYPE(*CHAR) LEN(512)
  1300          DCL        VAR(&SAVED) TYPE(*LGL) LEN(1) VALUE('0')
  1400
  1500          MONMSG     MSGID(CPF0000) EXEC(GOTO CMDLBL (ERROR))
  1600
  1700          RTVDTAARA  DTAARA(*LDA (1 512)) RTNVAR(&BUFFER)
  1800          CHGVAR     VAR(&SAVED) VALUE('1')
  1900
  2000          SBMJOB     JOB(PGM001) JOBD(&JOBD) RQSDTA('call pgm001')
  2100
  2200          SNDPGMMSG  MSG('batch job PGM001 submitted...')
  2300
  2400 ERROR:
  2500          RCVMSG     RMV(*NO) MSG(&MSG) MSGDTA(&MSGDTA) +
  2600                       MSGID(&MSGID) /* receive message from +
  2700                       program message queue */
  2800
  2900          IF         COND(&MSG *NE ' ') THEN(DO)
  3000          IF         COND(%SST(&MSGID 1 3) *NE 'CPF') THEN(DO)
  3100          SNDPGMMSG  MSG(&MSG) MSGTYPE(*DIAG)
  3200          MONMSG     MSGID(CPF0000)
  3300          ENDDO
  3400          ELSE       CMD(DO)
  3500          SNDPGMMSG  MSGID(&MSGID) MSGF(QCPFMSG) MSGDTA(&MSGDTA) +
  3600                       MSGTYPE(*DIAG) /* send message from +
  3700                       system message file */
  3800          MONMSG     MSGID(CPF0000)
  3900          ENDDO
  4000          GOTO       CMDLBL(ERROR)
  4100          ENDDO
  4200          SNDPGMMSG  MSG('program ended abnormally') MSGTYPE(*DIAG)
  4300          MONMSG     MSGID(CPF0000)
  4400          IF         COND(&SAVED) THEN(CHGDTAARA DTAARA(*LDA (1 +
  4500                       512)) VALUE(&BUFFER)
  4600          ENDPGM

                     * * * * END OF SOURCE * * * *
```

Figure 8.2.

8.4.2. Message Queue That Gets the Message

The predefined values for the program message queue can be:

- *PRV (previous)
- *SAME (same)
- *EXT (external)

If you have specified *PRV as the program message queue, the message is sent to the program message queue associated with the program that called the current program. On the other hand, if you specify *SAME as the program message queue, the message is sent to the current program's program message queue. If you specify *EXT as the destination, then the current job's message queue receives the message.

From the diagrams in Figures 8.3 and 8.4, we can see that the program stack determines which message queue gets the message.

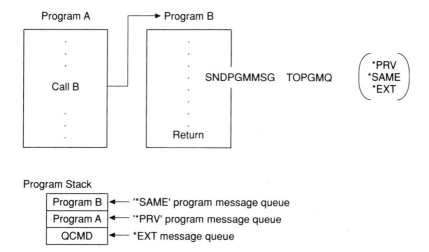

Figure 8.3.

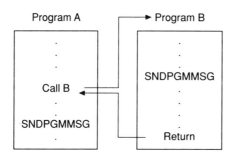

	Program A	Program B
*PRV	QCMD	A's program message queue
*SAME	A's program message queue	B's program message queue
*EXT	QCMD	QCMD

Figure 8.4.

The TOPGMQ parameter can also accept a second value that indicates what program message queue in the program stack will receive the message. If the named program was called more than once, its name will appear more than once in the stack; then the message is sent to the most recent one, for example, if program A calls program B, program B then calls program C. If we send a message in program C as follows:

```
SNDPGMMSG ........ TOPGMQ(*PRV) or
SNDPGMMSG ........ TOPGMQ(*SAME B)
```

then both messages are sent to program B. However, if the statement is as follows:

```
SNDPGMMSG ......... TOPGMQ(*PRV B)
```

then the message is sent to program A.

Tips

Go through these points before you send a message:

1. Is it an impromptu, program-described, or predefined message?
   If it is a predefined message, are the message descriptions already defined?
2. Where do you want to send the message?
   Permanent or temporary message queue? And which one?
3. What type of message do you want?
   The message type will be determined by the MSGTYP parameter.
4. Do you expect a reply?
   If so, how are you going to receive it?

8.5. Message Types

The message type indicates the mode of delivery of the message and it is specified in the send message commands. The following are the valid message types on the AS/400; however, not all of them are allowed for a particular send message command. For example, the Send Break Message (SNDBRKMSG) command only delivers the message in break (*INQ) mode and informational (*INFO) mode.

8.5.1. Inquiry (*INQ)

An inquiry message is delivered to the receiver in break mode. The display station screen is interrupted and a prompt screen is displayed so that the receiver of the message has to enter a reply to the message. The reply that the receiver enters is sent back to the sender of the message as a Reply Message (*RPY). An inquiry message is sent to the external message queue of the current job most of the time.

8.5.2. Notify (*NOTIFY)

We can implement a notify message in our CL program to notify the user that a certain error condition has happened and prompt the user for a reply. The notify message type is only valid when the message is sent to a program message queue or the external queue of the current job; you cannot send to any permanent message queue. The following statement shows you how to send a message as a notify message with the SNDPGMMSG command:

```
SNDPGMMSG MSGID(.....) MSGF(.....) MSGDTA(&VAR1) +
   MSGTYPE(*NOTIFY)
```

The program sending the notify message ends immediately.

8.5.3. Informational (*INFO)

An informational message can be sent by any send command and to any kind of message queue. The message is for informational purposes only and does not require any reply. The following statement shows you how to send a message as an informational message with the SNDPGMMSG command:

```
SNDPGMMSG MSGID(.....) MSGF(.....) MSGDTA(&VAR1) +
   MSGTYPE(*INFO)
```

8.5.4. Status (*STATUS)

We can implement the send message command in our CL program to send a status message reporting the progress of the program on the screen of the display station. This kind of status message can only be sent to the program message queues or to the external message queue of the current job. If sent to the external message queue of a current job, the message appears at the bottom of the screen. If the message is sent to a program message queue, the receiving program can receive the message and take appropriate action in response to status.

8.5.5. Escape (*ESCAPE)

Escape messages are sent to a program message queue informing the user that the program or command was terminated abnormally. The program or command that sends the escape message ends immediately after the message is sent. In the receiving program we can monitor any kind of escape messages and determine appropriate actions to be taken. The following statement shows you how to send a message as an escape message with the SNDPGMMSG command:

```
SNDPGMMSG MSGID(.....) MSGF(.....) MSGDTA(&VAR1) +
   MSGTYPE(*ESCAPE)
```

The program that sends the escape message ends immediately.

Tip

The main difference between an escape message and a notify message is that the escape message describes an unrecoverable error; a notify message describes an error that can be corrected.

8.5.6. Completion (*COMP)

You can send a completion message to any kind of message queue upon the successful completion of the command or program. The following statement shows you how to send a message as a completion message with the SNDPGMMSG command:

```
SNDPGMMSG MSGID(.....) MSGF(.....) MSGDTA(&VAR1) +
   MSGTYPE(*COMP)
```

8.5.7. Diagnostic (*DIAG)

You can send diagnostic messages to any kind of message queue upon the detection of any error conditions encountered while running a command or program. The following statement shows you how to send a message as a diagnostic message with the SNDPGMMSG command:

```
SNDPGMMSG MSGID(.....) MSGF(.....) MSGDTA(&VAR1) +
    MSGTYPE (*DIAG)
```

8.5.8. Reply (*RPY)

As mentioned before, when the message is sent to the receiver in break mode it expects the receiver to reply to the message on the prompt screen, and the reply that is entered is then sent back to the message sender as a reply message. You can specify which message queue the reply message will be stored in when you send the message in break mode.

8.5.9. Request (*RQS)

Every time a user enters a command, the command is sent to the external message queue of the current job. The system receives the message from the message queue and processes it. This receiving mechanism is handled by a special system program — QCMD.

The SNDPGMMSG command sends the messages to the current job's program message queue in all cases above. However, if the destination is a permanent message queue, you need to do a DSPMSG command to see the messages.

The table in Figure 8.5 shows that you can send any kind of messages to a program message queue except inquiry messages (*INQ), and you can send any kind of messages to a permanent message queue except status messages (*STATUS).

	Program Message Queue	Permanent Message Queue
*INFO	Yes	Yes
*INQ	No	Yes
*RQS	Yes	Yes
*COMP	Yes	Yes
*DIAG	Yes	Yes
*NOTIFY	Yes	Yes
*ESCAPE	Yes	Yes
*STATUS	Yes	No

Figure 8.5.

8.6. How to Receive a Message

8.6.1. Using RCVMSG to Receive a Message

We use the Receive Message (RCVMSG) command to receive any messages from a message queue and return its value into a CL program variable. Since messages can be sent to either permanent or temporary message queues, the RCVMSG command can receive messages selectively from both permanent and temporary message queues. After the message is received by the RCVMSG command, the message id, message text, and message data can be placed into CL program variables.

When you receive a message using the RCVMSG command, you can indicate whether this command will receive a message from a permanent or temporary message queue. If you want to receive a message from a permanent message queue, you can specify the message queue in the MSGQ parameter. If you want to receive a message from a temporary message queue, you can indicate that in the PGMQ parameter. Of course these two parameters are mutually exclusive and you can only specify one of them.

It is easiest when you want to specify a permanent message queue. You just enter the permanent message queue and the library name in the MSGQ parameter.

When you want to receive a message from either an external message queue or program message queue, you can enter one of the following predefined values in the PGMQ parameter:

1. First element = *SAME, second element = *
   The RCVMSG command receives a message from the current program's program message queue.
2. First element = *SAME, second element = name of a program
   The RCVMSG command receives a message from the named program's program message queue.
3. First element = *PRV, second element = *
   The RCVMSG command receives a message from the program message queue of the program that called the current program.
4. First element = *PRV, second element = name of a program
   The RCVMSG command receives a message from the program message queue of the program that called the named program.

5. First element = *EXT, second element = *
   The RCVMSG command receives a message from the external message queue of the current program.

The program in Figure 8.6 shows you how to combine the SNDBRKMSG and the RCVMSG commands in your application.

In this program, it will send a break message to the workstation message queue and prompt the user for an answer; press the <ENTER> key to continue or enter a "C" to cancel the job. Then the RCVMSG command in the program receives the answer from the workstation message queue and determines whether it should abort the program or go on to run the Copy to Tape (CPYTOTAP) command. If any error occurs with the CPYTOTAP command a break message is sent to the workstation message queue and advises the user to display the contents of the tape to determine what went wrong.

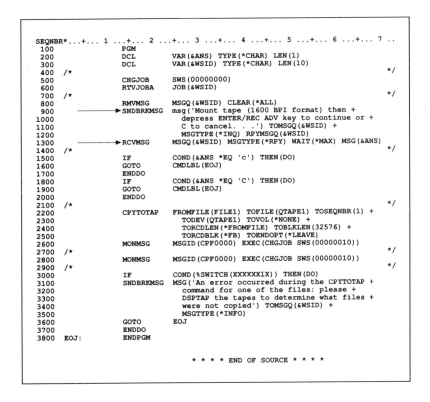

```
SEQNBR*...+... 1 ...+... 2 ...+... 3 ...+... 4 ...+... 5 ...+... 6 ...+... 7 ..
  100            PGM
  200            DCL        VAR(&ANS) TYPE(*CHAR) LEN(1)
  300            DCL        VAR(&WSID) TYPE(*CHAR) LEN(10)
  400    /*                                                               */
  500            CHGJOB     SWS(00000000)
  600            RTVJOBA    JOB(&WSID)
  700    /*                                                               */
  800            RMVMSG     MSGQ(&WSID) CLEAR(*ALL)
  900          ->SNDBRKMSG  msg('Mount tape (1600 BPI format) then +
 1000                       depress ENTER/REC ADV key to continue or +
 1100                       C to cancel. . .') TOMSGQ(&WSID) +
 1200                       MSGTYPE(*INQ) RPYMSGQ(&WSID)
 1300          ->RCVMSG     MSGQ(&WSID) MSGTYPE(*RPY) WAIT(*MAX) MSG(&ANS)
 1400    /*                                                               */
 1500            IF         COND(&ANS *EQ 'c') THEN(DO)
 1600            GOTO       CMDLBL(EOJ)
 1700            ENDDO
 1800            IF         COND(&ANS *EQ 'C') THEN(DO)
 1900            GOTO       CMDLBL(EOJ)
 2000            ENDDO
 2100    /*                                                               */
 2200            CPYTOTAP   FROMFILE(FILE1) TOFILE(QTAPE1) TOSEQNBR(1) +
 2300                       TODEV(QTAPE1) TOVOL(*NONE) +
 2400                       TORCDLEN(*FROMFILE) TOBLKLEN(32576) +
 2500                       TORCDBLK(*FB) TOENDOPT(*LEAVE)
 2600            MONMSG     MSGID(CPF0000) EXEC(CHGJOB SWS(00000010))
 2700    /*                                                               */
 2800            MONMSG     MSGID(CPF0000) EXEC(CHGJOB SWS(00000010))
 2900    /*                                                               */
 3000            IF         COND(%SWITCH(XXXXXX1X)) THEN(DO)
 3100            SNDBRKMSG  MSG('An error occurred during the CPYTOTAP +
 3200                       command for one of the files; please +
 3300                       DSPTAP the tapes to determine what files +
 3400                       were not copied') TOMSGQ(&WSID) +
 3500                       MSGTYPE(*INFO)
 3600            GOTO       EOJ
 3700            ENDDO
 3800    EOJ:    ENDPGM


              * * * * END OF SOURCE * * * *
```

Figure 8.6.

8.6.2. How to Implement the RCVMSG Command

One thing to bear in mind is the timing of the execution of the RCVMSG command.

If the RCVMSG command is run before the expected message is sent, then it receives nothing from the message queue. Therefore we need to implement some kind of looping mechanism so that when the RCVMSG command receives nothing, it waits for a certain period of time and then goes back to the message queue looking for messages. This looping will continue until the message is received successfully.

The RCVMSG command provides the WAIT parameter, which specifies how long (in seconds) it will wait until going back to the message queue looking for messages. The valid values that you can specify include: 0, any numeric allowed by the system, and the predefined value *MAX. If you specify 0, this command would not wait for any message and go to the next command if no message is received. If you specify *MAX, it would wait indefinitely until a message is received. If you specify a value expressed in seconds, it would wait for that amount of time for a message, if no message is received by the program.

8.6.3. Message Retrieval and Message Queue

The message queue is an object organized in the First-In-First-Out manner. Therefore, if we do not specify any value in the message key (MSGKEY) parameter in the RCVMSG command, messages are received in the default manner (First-In-First-Out).

We can combine and use both the message key and the message type to receive the kind of message we want. For example, if we specify *INFO as the message type and specify *NONE as the message key, then the informational message that arrives at the message queue first is received by the command. On the other hand, if we know the value of the message key, we can specify its value in the MSGKEY parameter, then the message that matches the specified message type and message key would be received into the CL program. Messages can be received by the RCVMSG command in the following ways.

8.6.3.1. Retrieve Message by Message Type

You can receive messages by message type by specifying one of the predefined values (*INFO, *INQ, *RPY, *NOTIFY, etc.) in the MSGTYPE parameter. Messages matching the specified message type are received by the program in the First-In-First-Out manner.

8.6.3.2. Retrieve Message by Message Key

You can receive messages by message key by specifying the value in the MSGKEY parameter. Messages whose message reference key, if any, match the specified value are received by the program.

8.6.3.3. Retrieve Message by Location

You can receive the first and the last message in the message queue by specifying MSGTYPE(*FIRST) or MSGTYPE(*LAST).

8.6.3.4. Retrieve Message by the Combination of Message Type and Message Key

The kind of information that you can receive from a message includes the following:

1. The value of the message key, if any
2. The first level of the message text
3. The second level of the message text, if any
4. The length of the first-level message text
5. The length of the second-level message text, if any
6. The message data for the embedded variables in a predefined message, if any
7. The length of the message data, if any
8. The message identification number, if the message is a predefined message
9. The severity code of the message
10. The user profile of the sender of the message
11. A numeric code that represents the message type

We can declare the necessary CL variables in our program for the RCVMSG command to receive this information from the message queue and store it in these program variables.

8.7. Monitor Message

8.7.1. What Is the Purpose of MONMSG?

The CL command Monitor Message (MONMSG) acts as an error trap in our CL programs.

Each CL command sends an error message to the program when it encounters an unexpected condition, but sometimes we do not want the program aborted or ended abnormally due to these "error" conditions. Therefore we specify the actions to be taken when these conditions occur. The mechanism used to trap these conditions is MONMSG.

Let's look at one example: we check for the existence of an object (use the CHKOBJ command) before we do anything to it and, if it does not exist, the CHKOBJ command sends back an error message to the program. However, we should expect that the object may not exist all the time. This is not really an "error" condition. Therefore, in the program logic, we should trap the error message sent by the CHKOBJ command. We can also specify the actions to be taken (for example, create such an object) when such an "error" condition occurs.

The syntax of the Monitor Message (MONMSG) command is as follows:

```
MONMSG MSGID(message-identifier) CMPDTA(comparison-data) +
   EXEC(CL-commands)
```

Of course, we need to think beforehand what kinds of error conditions may occur when a particular command is run, and find out the corresponding error messages that could be sent by the system. There is a complete list of error messages that can be monitored for each CL command in the Reference Manual provided by IBM, and most of them are escape messages. For example, for the CHKOBJ command, the most often encountered error message is CPF9801, which means object not found. If we have decided what to do if the object is not found, we can implement the CHKOBJ and MONMSG command statements in our program as follows:

```
PGM
 .
 .
CHKOBJ OBJ(object-name)
MONMSG MSGID(CPF9801) EXEC(DO)
 .
 .
actions
```

```
          .
          .
   ENDDO
          .
          .
   ENDPGM
```

8.7.2. Types of MONMSG

The MONMSG command can be executed at the program level or at the command level. The placement of the MONMSG command determines whether it is a program-level or command-level MONMSG.

When we monitor an error message at the program level, the error is taken care of any time it happens. When we monitor an error message at the command level, the error is taken care of only when the particular command that causes it is run.

When we want to implement the MONMSG command at the program level, we can code the MONMSG command immediately after the last DCL statements, or when there are no DCL statements, immediately after the PGM statement. To implement a MONMSG command at the command level, we can code the MONMSG command immediately after the command that we want to monitor.

We can monitor messages either specifically or generically. As mentioned above, message identification numbers consist of 7 characters in which the first one must be alphabetic, followed by two alphanumeric, and the remaining four can be any digits or characters. So, the message id would look like this in general:

```
pppnnnn
```

When you want to monitor only one specific message, you can specify the message id to be monitored to be pppnnnn; for example CPF3426, the MONMSG statement in your CL program, would be:

```
MONMSG     MSGID(CPF3426)
```

However, if you want to monitor a range of message id, then you can specify the message id with wildcard representations, that is, pppnn00 or pp0000; for example, if you want to monitor the range of messages from CPF3410 to CPF3499, you can code the MONMSG statement as follows:

```
MONMSG     MSGID(CPF3400)
```

If you want to monitor all messages with message id always starting with CPF, your MONMSG statement should look like this:

```
MONMSG     MSGID(CPF0000)
```

The 00 and 0000 in the above two MONMSG statements actually act as wildcard characters representing the generic names.

If we apply a MONMSG command to all error messages at the program level, the program is never interrupted for any reason. However, we have to think carefully about the advantages of doing this because some of the error messages are necessary for us to know the situation of the program. And sometimes the program really needs to be interrupted and an error condition has to be corrected before it goes any further.

8.8. Send Reply

The Send Reply (SNDRPY) command can be implemented in a CL program and run by batch; it cannot run at interactive mode. The function of it is to send a reply to an inquiry message that was sent to a permanent message queue. You must enter the message key and the name of the permanent message queue.

You can code your SNDRPY statement as follows:

```
SNDRPY MSGKEY(&msgkey) MSGQ(message-queue) RPY('Y')
```

if you want to send a reply to the inquiry message with message key &msgkey, which resides in the permanent message queue.

8.9. Message Logging

Messages can be recorded and written to log file. There are two kinds of message log files:

1. Job log
2. History log

For every job active on the system, the system creates a job log for it so that request messages sent to the job are recorded. The job log for the job records every command entered at the system command line and sent to the job for execution through external message queue, every command coded in a CL program, and every message sent to program message queues during the lifetime of the job.

You can control the level of detail that is written to the job log by changing the LOG parameter in the Change Job Description

(CHGJOBD) or Change Job (CHGJOB) commands. There are three components within the LOG parameter: message level, severity level, and message text level.

There are five levels for the message level that you can choose:

Level 0 — no message is logged

Level 1 — only logs messages sent to the external message queue whose severity level is equal to or greater than the severity level specified

Level 2 — includes level 1 messages and commands of a CL program and messages associated with these commands and whose severity level is equal to or greater than the severity level specified

Level 3 — includes level 2 messages and messages sent to program message queues whose severity level is equal to or greater than the severity level specified

Level 4 — includes commands coded in CL programs and messages whose severity level is equal to or greater than the severity level specified

The severity level is the minimum condition in which error messages are sent to the job log. It is a 2-digit value ranging from 00 to 99. Any messages whose severity level is greater than the specified severity level would be recorded onto the job log. The values of the severity level are predefined by IBM.

Tip

If you do not want the low-severity messages added to the job message queue, change the second element (severity level) in the LOG parameter in the CHGJOB command.

The message text level has three predefined values that you can specify:

*NOLIST — no job log is produced if the job ends normally. Usually if the job is ended abnormally, the system produces a job log and stores it in the output queue as a spooled file.

*SECLVL — both first- and second-level message texts would be written to the job log.

*MSG — only message text would be written to the job log; help text would be excluded.

When the job is ended, either normally or abnormally, you can write the job log to a spooled file and store it in an output queue. If you do not write the job log to a spooled file when the job is ended, you will not be able to retrieve its information in the future, because when a job is ended the job log is also deleted by the system.

Job log can be displayed while the job is still active on the system; you can use the Display Job Log (DSPJOBLOG) command to display the job log recorded so far:

```
DSPJOBLOG
```

Then it displays your current job's job log. You can see that the entire history of your job is recorded as messages. Even the commands you type in are messages.

If you want to display another job's job log, you have to specify the job name in the DSPJOBLOG command:

```
DSPJOBLOG 123456/user1/dsp01
```

The history log is a special object with name QHST. It is maintained by the system and contains information regarding system activities, for example, log-on and log-off information, starting and ending of subsystems, starting and ending of jobs, device activities and messages sent to the system operator message queue, and so forth.

You can send messages to QHST to enhance application auditing. In your CL program you can implement a send message command as follows:

```
SNDMSG MSG('..........') TOMSGQ(QHST)
```

This records the message onto the history log. You can later display the contents of the history log by the Display Log (DSPLOG) command.

You can also process information contained in the history log by displaying its contents into a spooled file. You need the information about the QHST file before you can code your program; you can find all this information in the IBM Reference Manual. Basically, you process the history log just as you would any other physical files. You can define the record on it as a data structure with a length of 142. The first 10 digits is the record number and the remaining is an array containing the system information. The array includes information such as job name, user name, job number, job start date and time, job type, and so forth.

8.10. System Reply List

The system reply list is a system object stored on the system. There are no commands to create or delete the system reply list, but you can add, change, or delete a reply list entry. You can display the reply list entries by using the Work with Reply List Entries (WRKRPYLE) command. Figure 8.7 is the display of the system reply list.

```
                      Work with System Reply List Entries
         Type options, press Enter.
           2=Change    4=Delete

         Opt   Sequence  Message                                        Compare
               Number    ID      Reply     Compare Value               Start
                   10    CPA0700  D         *NONE
                   20    CPA5305  I         *NONE
                   30    CBE0000  D         *NONE
                   40    PLI0000  D         *NONE
                  955    CPA5737  C         MPGLIN    MPGCTL             6
                 1955    CPA5737  C         MPGLIN    MPGCTL             6


                                                                       Bottom

         Parameters or command
         ===>
         F3=Exit    F5=Refresh    F6=Add    F11=Display entire reply    F12=Cancel
         F24=More keys
         (C) COPYRIGHT IBM CORP. 1980, 1991.
```

Figure 8.7. System reply list entries display.

Any reply list entries include the sequence number, a 7-character identifier, a compare value of 28 bytes in length, a compare start position that ranges from 1 to 999, and the automatic reply value that can be up to 32 bytes long. You can add any reply list entry by using the Add Reply List Entry (ADDRPYLE) command.

If you expect an error to occur in your program, you can implement your program so that it reads from the system reply list to get the reply value for any *INQ or *NOTIFY messages it receives. This is handy especially when your program is running unattended.

Command Summary

CRTMSGQ	Create Message Queue
DSPMSG	Display Messages
CHGMSGQ	Change Message Queue
CLRMSGQ	Clear Message Queue

CRTMSGF	Create Message File
ADDMSGD	Add Message Descriptions
SNDPGMMSG	Send Program Message
SNDMSG	Send Message
SNDUSRMSG	Send User Message
SNDBRKMSG	Send Break Message
SNDNETMSG	Send Network Message
RCVMSG	Receive Message
MONMSG	Monitor Message
SNDRPY	Send Reply
DSPJOBLOG	Display Job Log
WRKRPYLE	Work with Reply List Entries

Exercises

8.1. What are the major types of message queues?

8.2. What are the steps to create a message description?

8.3. What commands can be used to send a message:
- from user to user
- from user to program
- from program to program

8.4. What is the difference between:
- an informational and an inquiry message
- a notify and an escape message

8.5. What commands are used to receive messages from a message queue?

8.6. What is the function of MONMSG? How could we find out the message id related to any CL command and identify it in the MONMSG command?

File Processing

This chapter first explains the basic concept of files on the AS/400; then the set of commands that manipulate them is examined in detail. Since the AS/400 has the unique concept of database and file, you have to understand these concepts before any file processing commands are learned.

You should understand that control language (CL) programs on the AS/400 are originally intended for system tasks and are not designed for commercial data processing purposes. Therefore, when we build applications on the AS/400, we use a CL program as the driver of the module to set up the running environment for the HLL programs. Most of the time, the CL program calls another HLL program to perform the data processing task.

CL commands on the AS/400 can do only very limited database file processing tasks. There is a command that sets a pointer to a database file and reads records sequentially from there, but there is no command that creates new records or updates existing records. Each CL program can declare only one database file. This chapter introduces these file processing commands on the AS/400.

9.1. What Is a File on the AS/400?

9.1.1. Types of Files

There are several file types on the AS/400:

9.1.1.1. Database File

Database files include physical files and logical files.

By definition, a file is an object with object type *FILE on the AS/400. A physical file is an object of object type *FILE and attribute PF; a logical file is an object of object type *FILE and attribute LF. A physical file is a kind of database file that contains data and can be created by the Create Physical File (CRTPF) command. On the other hand, a logical file does not really store any data at all and is created by the Create Logical File (CRTLF) command. Logical files are actually the index of the data stored in physical files; we can use a logical file to access the data in a physical file.

A file comes into existence when it is created by the appropriate system command. They are stored in a library and occupy storage space. Each file has a set of file descriptions associated with it. File descriptions are information that describes the characteristics of the file. It is an integral part of the file and remains with the file until the file is deleted. The collection of file descriptions is the declaration of the valid operations for the file and also determines how a program can use the data or devices. If the program tries to perform an operation not consistent with the file descriptions the operation will not be allowed. You can display the file description with the Display File Descriptions (DSPFD) command.

```
DSPFD FILE(file-name)
```

Some of the more important attributes of the file include:

1. Type of file (physical file, logical file, display file, etc.)
2. Is it externally described? (means that the field definitions of the record layout are defined in a Data Description Specification source)
3. File level identifier
4. Maximum number of members allowed
5. Current number of members
6. Access path maintenance method
7. Maximum size of member
8. Is level check enforced?
9. Is unique key required?
10. Number of key fields
11. Names of the key fields
12. Number of fields in each record

13. Record length
14. Creation date of the member and file
15. Current number of records on file
16. Date last used

Physical and logical files are database files and they provide a place to store data and the access path to the database. Database files are accessed in a certain way, for example, by index or sequentially. The database files must be processed according to the file format defined, for example, you cannot retrieve any record randomly by key from a sequential file that has no key fields assigned. On the other hand, you can access a physical file through a logical file, which defines how the records in the physical file are accessed and arranged.

When either a physical or logical file is opened for processing, a data path is built and any access to the file is through that data path. A file pointer is returned to the program upon the opening of the file. The file pointer is always pointing at the record for the next processing step. Therefore, when you access an indexed file with a key, the file pointer should be pointing at the record matching the key value. On the other hand, when you open a sequential file for processing, the file pointer should be pointing at the first record upon the successful opening of the file.

Tip

A physical file is the place to store data and a logical file is the logical view of it.

9.1.1.2. Device File

The Device file contains the definitions of how to use a physical device, such as the display station, printer, tape device, and so forth. The definitions contained in a device file describe how the physical device should behave and what functions it is supposed to perform under certain situations. Although a device file is regarded as a kind of file, it doesn't really contain any permanent data at all. A device file that associates with the display station is called a display file (object type *FILE with attribute DSPF). See Figure 9.1.

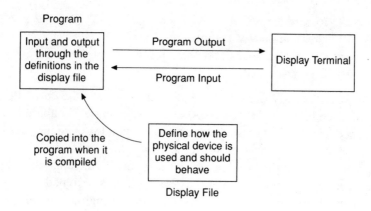

Figure 9.1. Device file and physical device.

Of course, the device file functions are restricted by the device descriptions associated with the physical device. For example, we can define in a display file function that a certain line on the screen can blink; however, the same kind of function is not applicable in a printer file function. Just as with a database file, a device file has to be opened before it can be used. Opening a device file involves establishing a path between the device and the program. The program can read/write data from/to the device through the path established, and the device file controls the data flow between the program and the device.

Tip

A device file defines how a physical device can be used.

9.1.1.3. DDM File

Distributed Data Management (DDM) files are employed when the AS/400 on which your current job is running tries to access data files on another AS/400.

The DDM file lets your program use data on another AS/400 just as it uses data files on your own machine. The DDM file accesses the target system (the other AS/400) from the source system (the AS/400 on which your job runs) through the communication line and reads the data file on the target system as determined in your program. Just as with any other database files, DDM files have to be opened before they can be used by your program. After the DDM file is opened, a path is established to access the target system; the data files reside on the target system. The DDM file serves as a medium connecting the program running on the source system and the database file on the target system, and by using the DDM file in your program you can manipulate the data files on the target system as if they were on the source system. The use of DDM files will get more popular in the future since the trend of the industry is networking; data will be shared among users on separate machines in the network.

By using DDM files you can:

- copy a file from the remote system to the local AS/400 system
- copy a file from the local AS/400 system to the remote system
- manage files residing on a remote system
- access data in the files residing on a remote system
  etc.

Figure 9.2 illustrates how to use a DDM file to communicate between the target system and the source system.

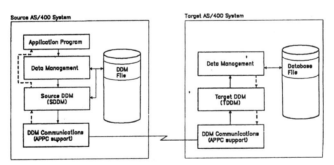

Figure 9.2. Communication using DDM file.

9.1.1.4. Save File

Save files are files used to contain data in a format for backup and recovery purposes. Save files can be used for data transfer. Figure 9.3 illustrates how we can use save files for backup and recovery purposes.

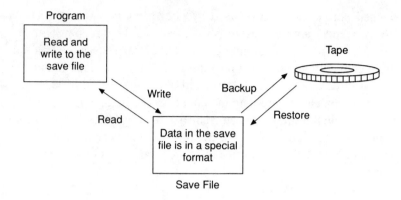

Figure 9.3. The use of save files.

We have already discussed the different types of files on the AS/400; however, in this chapter we will primarily concentrate on database files: physical and logical files.

9.1.2. How to Create a File

First of all, we define the field definitions for the record layout using the Data Description Specification (DDS) source and then create the file by compiling the DDS. This kind of file is called an externally described file, since the detailed descriptions of the file exist outside the program and are associated with the file itself.

The Data Description Specification (DDS) is the source for the file descriptions and can be compiled. In the DDS the record format is the logical description of the physical record; it describes how the group of fields are organized into the record. Therefore, the fields and records are not defined within the program. The record format for the physical file as shown in Figure 9.4 describes how the fields appear in the record. From the DDS, we can see that the file has seven fields in each record; these fields appear in the same order as shown in the DDS. Their data types are also defined in the DDS. Record formats are stored in the file descriptions. In your HLL programs, you can access the database file by specifying either the file name or the record format name. You can also define more than one record format for each physical file.

We can also create a physical file without using the DDS and, if that is the case, we do not need to specify the source file and the member name in the CRTPF command. However, we need to specify the record length for the file. Once the physical file is created, we can describe the record layout inside our HLL program and assign field names as well. This kind of file processing is called a program-described file. A program-described file is a file created by CRTPF command without using DDS. You specify the field names of the file inside your program.

Figure 9.4 shows the DDS for the file.

```
                                                            01/27/93 09:36:

SEQNBR*...+... 1 ...+... 2 ...+... 3 ...+... 4 ...+... 5 ...+... 6 ...+... 7 ...+...
  100      A           R RCDFMT                      TEXT('CUSTOMER MASTER FILE')
  200      A             CUSNUM         6  0          TEXT('CUSTOMER NUMBER')
  300      A             CUSNAM        10A            TEXT('CUSTOMER NAME')
  400      A             ADDRES        30A            TEXT('CUSTOMER ADDRESS')
  500      A             PHONE#        10A            TEXT('TELEPHONE NUMBER')
  600      A             CUSTYP         1A            TEXT('CUSTOMER TYPE')
  700      A             ARBAL          6  2          TEXT('ACCOUNT RECEIVABLE AMOUNT')
  800      A             INVDAT         6  0          TEXT('INVOICE DATE')

                    * * * * END OF SOURCE * * * *
```

Figure 9.4. DDS for a physical file.

After the Data Description Specification is coded for the physical file, we can create the physical file by compiling the DDS using the Create Physical File (CRTPF) command. The CRTPF command compiles the DDS source into executable code; upon the successful compilation of the DDS source, a compiled object is produced and placed in a library. The CRTPF command includes the following parameters:

1. File name
2. Source file name
3. Source member name
4. Member name
5. Maximum number of members allowed

Each DDS is stored in a source physical file as a member. When you want to create a physical file by using the CRTPF command, you must specify where the compiler can find the source code for the physical file. The source physical file has many members in it, and each member contains the source code for an individual physical file.

The newly created physical file object will have an unlimited number of members (since the MAXMBRS parameter is specified as *NOMAX), and the first member will have the same name as the physical file itself (since the parameter mbr is *FILE).

There are many other attributes that we can supply when we create the physical file. The more important ones include:

1. Maximum number of members
2. Access path maintenance method
3. Maximum size of a member
4. Whether the open data path is shared by other programs in the same job
5. Whether level check is enforced
6. Authorities for the other users

9.1.3. What Is a Member?

A member is a subset of the data records of the physical file. All the records in a physical file can be in one member or can be grouped into several members. Each member of the file has to conform to the same characteristics and attributes of the file, including the record format and file descriptions. Each member has its associated data and its own access path. The system creates and maintains an access path for each member.

When creating the physical file, you can specify the number of members allowed in the physical file. The first member of the file is the default member for use in any program. Your program performs operations on the first member of the file as default, unless another member is explicitly specified by your program.

You can explicitly specify which member to use by the Override Database File (OVRDBF) command in your CL program. The statement below shows you how to override the first member with the specified member:

```
OVRDBF FILE(file-name) TOFILE(file-name) MBR(member-name)
```

Any subsequent HLL programs called by the CL program use the overriding member instead of the first member for file processing, until the override is deleted.

Each member has its own set of data records. Some applications make use of members for data organization purposes. For example, transaction records are created each month when a certain function is run. These records for different fiscal years can be stored in one single member or in separate members in the physical file. If the decision is to store all records in one member, then the record layout should include an extra field identifying the fiscal year. The disadvantage of this design is that the performance will degrade when the member size grows. On the other hand, if data records are stored in separate members, the fiscal year field can be eliminated and the size of each member would be small, thus resulting in better performance.

You can add new members to an existing physical file by the Add Physical member (ADDPFM) command. The ADDPFM command has the following syntax:

```
ADDPFM FILE(library-name/file-name) MBR(member-name)
         SHARE(*YES)
```

The FILE parameter in the ADDPFM command can be the qualified name of the physical file. The member name is the name of the new member that you want to add. Member name must be unique in the same physical file. The SHARE parameter specifies whether an open data path to the physical file will be shared with other programs in the same job.

Each member of the file is uniquely identified by its member name. The maximum number of members that can be added to the physical file is determined by the parameter MAXMBRS in the file descriptions.

9.1.4. Open Data Path

We have come across the term open data path in the previous section. An open data path for a file is the path through which all input and output operations on that file are performed.

The open data path connects the program to a file. An open data path does not contain any records at all; it only contains pointers to the actual records in the file, indicating which records to retrieve and in what order. An open data path is built whenever a file is opened by any particular program. The AS/400 operating system allows more than one program to share the same path to the data file or device. Each file-opening operation would create a new data path from the program to the data file or device. However, when you first open the file you can specify that the open data path would be shared with any other programs active in the same job, and if you make the data path available to the other programs in the same job, the other programs do not need to build their own data path since the active ODP can be reused, thus saving the amount of time required to open the file after the first "open." The amount of main storage required by the same job can be reduced as well. Therefore sharing an open data path allows more than one program to share the file status, positions, and storage area for the same file, and system performance will be remarkably improved.

You can design your application to do a "shared open" on a database file. However, you have to make sure that when the shared file is opened for the first time, all the open options that are needed by the other subsequent programs are also specified.

Another thing you need to be careful of is that the operating system uses the same input and output area for all programs sharing that file. When a program has done a shared open to a file and read a record from it and then calls another program, the called program does not open another data path and will read the record being pointed to by the called program. Therefore the file pointer created by the calling program is used by the called program, which reads the record being pointed to by the calling program.

9.1.5. What Is a Logical File?

A logical file is the logical view of a physical file. It provides an access path to the data in the physical file.

A logical file is like an index to a database table. You can define the logical file in the Data Description Specification source as well. See Figure 9.5.

```
                                                          01/27/93 09:36:

SEQNBR*...+... 1 ...+... 2 ...+... 3 ...+... 4 ...+... 5 ...+... 6 ...+... 7 ...+...
   100      A          R CUSFMT                    PFILE(FILE1)
   200      A          R CUSNUM

                    * * * * END OF SOURCE * * * *
```

Figure 9.5. DDS for a logical file.

The keyword PFILE specifies which physical file this logical view will be built upon. Therefore this logical file is dependent upon physical file FILE1. This logical file defines CUSNUM as a key field and thus provides access to the physical file FILE1 by specifying the value for the key field CUSNUM.

Logical files are created by compiling the DDS using the Create Logical File (CRTLF) command. The CRTLF command includes the following parameters:

1. File name
2. Source file name
3. Source member name
4. Member name
5. Maximum number of members
6. Access path maintenance method
7. Share open data path
8. Level check enforced

The CRTLF statement creates a logical file based on the data description specification source.

There are three types of access path maintenance:

1. Immediate (*IMMED)

   The access path for the logical file member is updated every time a physical file record is updated on the physical file. Therefore the logical file always reflects the real-time situation of the physical file. The disadvantage is the overhead involved. If the physical file has several logical files dependent upon it, then every time a record is updated to the physical file, changes have to be updated to the access path as well. If performance is an issue, try to avoid immediate update to the access path.

   In addition, if the file is keyed access, you must specify *IMMED for access path maintenance so that every time a new record is added to the physical file the system can see if the key value is duplicated.

2. Rebuild (*REBLD)

   As mentioned above, *IMMED is for access path maintenance that requires unique key values, and *REBLD is for access path maintenance that does not require unique key values. The access path for the logical file member is completely rebuilt when the logical file is opened, and the maintenance of the access path is continuously done until the logical file is closed.

3.　Delay (*DLY)

A delay maintenance of access path is for those access paths that do not require unique key values. The maintenance of the access path is delayed until the logical file member is opened. The changes that are updated to the access path are those changes made since the file was last opened.

Another important parameter in the CRTLF command is the SHARE parameter, which specifies whether the open data path for the logical file member is shared with other programs in the same job.

The Level Checked (LVLCHK) parameter specifies whether the record formats of the logical file are verified to be the same as specified in the program that opens the logical file.

Theoretically, we can create as many logical views on a physical file as we want. It all depends on how we want to design our application. However, we should always remember that logical files are actually an overhead, since every time we make an update to the physical file, all the logical files have to be updated as well. To lower the overhead, we can build the logical files that we want at program runtime and delete them when the program is finished. Try to avoid building a long composite key in the logical view.

Tips

1. Build the logical view at runtime to avoid extra overhead.
2. Avoid a long composite key.

When you want to create a keyed logical file, you need the object management and object operational authority to the physical file upon which you want to create the logical file.

The CRTLF command creates a logical file with the first member having the same name as the logical file itself. The first logical file member is also the default logical file member that any program performs operations upon, unless any other member is explicitly specified in the program. We can always add more members to the logical file with the Add Logical File Member (ADDLFM) command, if the maximum number of members allowed is more than one in the file descriptions.

The Display Database Relations (DSPDBR) command shows you all the logical views built upon a physical file.

Tip

The DSPDBR command can write the physical-logical file relations to an output file.

9.1.6. Other Commands Related to File

The following subsections will introduce you to some other commands that deal with physical files. These commands can either be
run at the command line interactively or be coded in CL programs
that are run by batch. When we need to set up the running environment for data processing, these physical file commands come in
handy.

9.1.6.1. Clear Physical File Member (CLRPFM)

The first command is the Clear Physical File Member (CLRPFM)
command.

The specified member in the physical file is cleared by this
command and any data contained in the specified member is removed, including the deleted records.

After the member is cleared, the record count parameter in the
file descriptions is reset to zero and the member size parameter is
reset to the minimum size allowed again. However, one thing you
should bear in mind is that any file overrides imposed by the
OVRDBF command are ignored by the CLRPFM command. Of
course, your user profile should have object management and the
deletion authority on the file object on which you want to clear. You
can clear the physical file member interactively by typing the command below:

```
CLRPFM FILE(file-name) MBR(member-name)
```

Then the system removes all the data contained in the specified
member in the physical file, and if you do not specify which member
to clear it would clear the first member as the default. This command
will not run successfully if the file object is being used and locked
by any other job.

It is good programming practice to implement a MONMSG
after the CLRPFM, since the user who runs this command may not
have the authority to the file, the file member may be in use, the file

may not be in the library list, or the file may not exist. The following
piece of program traps these error conditions:

```
PGM
    .
    .
CLRPFM FILE(*LIBL/file name) MBR(*FIRST)
MONMSG MSGID(CPF3137 CPF3130 CPF3142) EXEC(DO)
SNDPGMMSG MSG('cannot clear file member, display job log
           for more +
           details') TOPGMQ(*PRV)
ENDDO
    .
    .
ENDPGM
```

9.1.6.2. Change Physical File (CHGPF)

Sometimes we need to change some of the attributes in the file descriptions, and we can do this by using the Change Physical File
(CHGPF) command. Some of the more important attributes that you
can change after the physical file is created include:

- Maximum number of members
- Access path maintenance method
- Member size
- Whether the open data path is shared
- Whether level check is enforced

The CHGPF command changes the attributes of all the file
members. That is to say, the changes are applicable to all its members. Any new members added to the physical file using the
ADDPFM command are conformed to these changes as well.

9.1.6.3. Change Physical File Member (CHGPFM)

On the other hand, if you want to change the attributes for only one
specific member, you should use the Change Physical File Member
(CHGPFM) command. In order to run this CHGPF and CHGPFM
command successfully in your CL programs, your user profile should
have the appropriate object management and operational authority
for the file. Before the CHGPF or CHGPFM command is executed,
either interactively or by batch, you should allocate the file object
for your exclusive use.

9.1.6.4. Display Physical File Member (DSPPFM)

There are several facilities you can use to display the contents in a physical file on the AS/400. The most straightforward way to do this is by using the Display Physical File Member (DSPPFM) command for displaying the data contents in the file member.

```
DSPPFM FILE(file-name)
```

The DSPPFM command displays the contents in a file member on an "as is" basis. The records are displayed in the arrival sequence in the file, which is exactly the physical arrangement of the records themselves in the file even though the file may be an indexed file. Also you would see some funny characters on the display; these are the numeric fields in packed format.

There are some other facilities that you can use to display the contents in the physical file member — for example, the Data File Utility (DFU), Query/400, SQL/400 — which convert the packed format of the numeric fields into a format that can be displayed and read by the user. Numeric fields are stored on the AS/400 in packed format mainly for storage economy. For example, a numeric field defined as 7 digits would occupy 7 bytes of storage when unpacked; however, it would only occupy 4 bytes when packed.

9.1.6.5. Reorganize Physical File Member (RGZPFM)

The command Reorganize Physical File Member (RGZPFM) removes deleted records from the file member and compresses the physical file in the database. In your program, you may delete a record from a file member; however, the data in the deleted record is erased from the file member but the record itself still occupies space in storage. These spaces would be released for use when the file member is reorganized.

Another advantage of the RGZPFM command is that if the file is an indexed file, the records are reshuffled to match the keyed sequence of the physical file access path or the access path of the logical file built upon the physical file, rather than the arrival sequence of the records. After a file member is reorganized, access to the records of the file will be more efficient and faster if any program uses a logical file or the keyed sequence for processing.

There is a KEYFILE parameter that you can specify in the RGZPFM command. This parameter, if specified, mainly indicates whether the arrival sequence of the records are rearranged to match the keyed sequence of the physical file member's access path, or the sequence as defined by a logical file definition; the deleted records are removed from the member as well. On the other hand, if the KEYFILE parameter is not specified at all, then no record rearrangement is furnished during reorganization and only the deleted records are removed.

When the RGZPFM command is in action, it does not care whether the file is being overridden. The command would reorganize the file member as specified in the FILE parameter. Of course, your user profile should have the necessary object operational and management authority to the file. While the RGZPFM command is performing action on the file object, it imposes some kind of object locking mechanism on the object so that no other user will be able to use it until the command is finished.

You can run RGZPGM on the relatively large transaction files in your application frequently, for example, weekly or monthly, for the sake of better system performance.

9.1.6.6. Rename Member (RNMM) and Remove Member (RMVM)

There are some other CL commands that you may need from time to time. These commands include the Rename Member (RNMM) command and the Remove Member (RMVM) command.

The RNMM command changes the name of the specified member in a file. You can rename a file using the Rename Object (RNMOBJ) command since each file is an object. However, a member is not an object and it is a subset of the data records of the file object. So if you want to rename a member, this command is the one you need.

The RMVM command removes the specified member from the physical file or logical file. All data contained in the member is lost once the member is removed.

9.1.6.7. Delete File (DLTF)

From time to time you may want to delete a physical file using the Delete File (DLTF) command in your CL programs according to the needs of your application design. This DLTF command would work on any database file and device file. However, in your program it should check on the database file relationship before any deletion of the physical file is done.

The command Display Database Relation (DSPDBR) would display the file dependencies. You can choose to display the result on screen, send to a spooled file for printing, or save in an output file. Since the existence of the logical files are all dependent on the physical file, the system does not allow you to delete a physical file without first deleting all the dependent logical files.

You may not be able to delete a file if one of the following occurs:

- File already deleted by another job
- Not authorized to the library that contains the file
- Not authorized to the object
- Not in the library list if qualified name is not used
- File being locked or allocated by another job

Tip

All logical views on the physical file must be deleted before it can be deleted.

9.2. CL Commands That Handle Files

We have already mentioned that CL commands are weak for commercial data processing since they are mainly intended for system administration tasks. Usually, we would use CL programs as the driver to set up the running environment for the HLL programs, which are called to perform the data processing tasks.

In CL programming, we have the following restrictions regarding file usage:

- Only one file can be declared in each CL program.
- The CL program can only read from the file declared record by record.
- The CL program cannot write to any database file, even if the file is declared in the program.
- The CL program can read and write to a display file declared in the program.

Before you can use any file in the CL program, you must first declare it. The command to declare a file is the Declare File (DCLF) command.

Only one DCLF command is allowed in each program. The DCLF command specifies the file and the record formats that are used in the program. By declaring the file in the program, the system allows us to interact with the file that is declared. Therefore the DCLF operation is very similar to the file-opening process in other HLL programs.

The declared file must exist when you compile your CL program. When the CL program is compiled, the compiler brings in the variables in the record formats declared. For example, if there is a field named FLD1 in the record format that was declared, the program would be able to use the variable &FLD1 and make reference to it in other commands. The data types of these variables are already defined in the Data Descriptions Specification of the file declared. We can use these variables just as we use any other program variables defined in the DCL commands in our program.

When using program-described files, you must extract the subfields every time you read a record from the file. Since there is no externally defined record format for a program-described file, the compiler treats each record in the file as consisting of a single field. That field is always named &file_name. You can extract the subfields you need to work with using the %SUBSTRING function.

Tip

Declare a file in the CL program with the DCLF command; only one DCLF statement is allowed in each program.

9.2.1. Commands That Send and Receive Data

The data manipulation commands that we can use in CL programming include the following.

9.2.1.1. Receive File (RCVF)

This command can read from both database and device files.

The RCVF command reads in the record and returns the data items into CL variables declared in the program. There is exactly one CL variable for every single field in the record format declared. The RCVF command only recognizes exactly one record format at one time; thus you cannot receive data from more than one record format. This is also a restriction of this command. The declared file is opened by the RCVF command when it runs and it does not use any open data path defined for the declared file.

9.2.1.2. Send File (SNDF)

This command can write to device files.

The SNDF command is used to send a record to a display file. The SNDF command sends the data contained in the CL program variables to the display file in the specified record format. Like the RCVF command, only one record format is recognized at one time. If the display file is not opened when the command runs, the SNDF command opens the display as well. Always remember that you cannot use the SNDF command to write a new record or update any existing record on a physical file.

9.2.1.3. Send/Receive File (SNDRCVF)

This command can write to and then read from device files.

The SNDRCVF command is used more often than RCVF and SNDF commands. However, the SNDRCVF command actually combines the functionalities of the other two. The SNDRCVF command sends data to a record format of the declared display file and then reads data from it and returns their values to the CL program variables.

The source codes in Figure 9.6 are the Data Description Specification of the menu display.

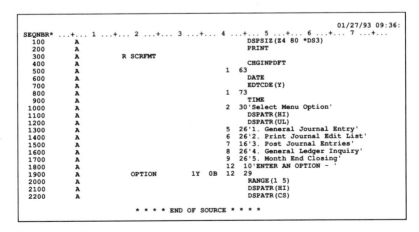

```
                                                                 01/27/93 09:36:
SEQNBR*  ...+... 1 ...+... 2 ...+... 3 ...+... 4 ...+... 5 ...+... 6 ...+... 7 ...+...
   100   A                                             DSPSIZ(Z4 80 *DS3)
   200   A                                             PRINT
   300   A         R SCRFMT
   400   A                                             CHGINPDFT
   500   A                                   1  63
   600   A                                             DATE
   700   A                                             EDTCDE(Y)
   800   A                                   1  73
   900   A                                             TIME
  1000   A                                   2  30'Select Menu Option'
  1100   A                                             DSPATR(HI)
  1200   A                                             DSPATR(UL)
  1300   A                                   5  26'1. General Journal Entry'
  1400   A                                   6  26'2. Print Journal Edit List'
  1500   A                                   7  16'3. Post Journal Entries'
  1600   A                                   8  26'4. General Ledger Inquiry'
  1700   A                                   9  26'5. Month End Closing'
  1800   A                                  12  10'ENTER AN OPTION - '
  1900   A         OPTION        1Y  0B     12  29
  2000   A                                             RANGE(1 5)
  2100   A                                             DSPATR(HI)
  2200   A                                             DSPATR(CS)

               * * * * END OF SOURCE * * * *
```

Figure 9.6. DDS for the menu display.

As we remember, the display file defines how the display device should behave. The CL program in Figure 9.7 declares that it is using the display file defined in the DDS.

```
                                                                    01/27/93 09:36:
SEQNBR* ...+... 1 ...+... 2 ...+... 3 ...+... 4 ...+... 5 ...+... 6 ...+... 7 ...+...
   100 PGM
   200              DCLF       FILE(SCREEN1)
   300  DISPLAY:    SNDRCVF    RCDFMT(SCRFMT)
   400              IF         COND(&OPTION = 1) THEN(CALL PGM(PGM123))
   500              ELSE       CMD(IF COND*&OPTION = 2) THEN(CALL +
   600                             PGM(PGM124)))
   700              ELSE       CMD(IF COND(&OPTION = 3) THEN(CALL +
   800                             PGM(PGM125)))
   900              ELSE       CMD(IF COND(&OPTION = 4) THEN(CALL +
  1000                             PGM(PGM126)))
  1100              ELSE       CMD(IF COND(&OPTION = 5) THEN(CALL +
  1200                             PGM(PGM127)))
  1300              ELSE       CMD(GOTO CMDLBL(DISPLAY))
  1400              ENDPGM

                        * * * * END OF SOURCE * * * *
```

Figure 9.7. CL program incorporating SNDRCVF.

This program uses the SNDRCVF command to write the display to the display device and then reads the input, the option number from the display, and returns its value to the variable &OPTION. The program calls other programs according to the value of &OPTION. If the user enters something other than 1 to 5, it will go to the SNDRCVF command again. This program is oversimplified since it does not incorporate any usage of indicators at all. Usually indicators, command keys, and error messages are implemented in the display file for better user interface.

Tip

Read the record from a database or device file into the program with RCVF; write to a display device with SNDF; write to the display device and read the user input with SNDRCVF.

9.2.2. File Override

File override is just another way of locating the file on the system and it is a way of making reference to a file in CL programs.

You can basically override any type of file: database file, device file, communication file, and so forth. As we remember, we can refer to a file by its qualified name; if the qualified name is not supplied, the system goes through the whole library list searching for the object with the same name.

File override is implemented in CL programs for the following reasons:

1. When the file that the application is looking for does not exist in any library in the library list, and we do not want to alter the current library list, we just use the Override Database File (OVRDBF) command to point to the location of the file. As shown below, the OVRDBF command overrides the file name specified in the FILE parameter with the qualified name specified in the TOFILE parameter. From then on, the program uses the value in the TOFILE parameter whenever any reference is made to the file name specified in the FILE parameter. Of course, we can always add a library to the library list by using the CHGLIBL command or ADDLIBLE command in the CL program. However, these commands create more overhead than does the OVRDBF command. So, OVRDBF command is the preferred way.

   ```
   OVRDBF FILE(file-name) TOFILE(library-name/file-name)
   ```

2. When the program wants to perform an action on a file member, it performs on the first member as the default. If we want to process a member other than the first one, we can also use the OVRDBF command to do it:

   ```
   OVRDBF FILE(file-name) MBR(member-name)
   ```

   This OVRDBF command overrides the default member, that is, the first member, with the member named in the MBR parameter.

3. CL programs can call other HLL programs and other HLL programs can call CL programs as well. However, the same file may be called differently in different programs. To overcome this problem, we can use the OVRDBF to override the name specified in other HLL programs with the name we use in the CL program.

   ```
   OVRDBF FILE(name-in-HLL-program) TOFILE(name-in-CL-
       program)
   ```

4. When the CL program wants to open a file and share its open data path (ODP) with other programs in the same job, you can make this level of sharing available by specifying the SHARE parameter on the OVRDBF command.

The file override remains in effect until the current program call level ends or the DLTOVR command is run. If you run an

OVRDBF command in a CL program that is called by another program, the file override will go away when the called program ends and control returns to the calling program.

Tip

OVRDBF will go away when the current CL program ends or when the DLTOVR is run.

9.3. How to Copy Data in a File

You can use a set of copying files commands to move data between databases and physical devices. On the AS/400, the following commands are available to copy data from device file to database file, from database file to device file, or from database file to database file.

9.3.1. The Copy File (CPYF) Command

The Copy File command has many uses. It can copy data and source code between database files. By using the CPYF command, records from physical or logical files can be copied to physical files. The CPYF command can also copy data from physical devices to databases and vice versa.

In the CPYF command, you can specify whether you want to copy all the data or just a portion of it. You can copy a range of records by specifying the starting and ending record number, or just the records matching the specified key values. You can set the criteria of choosing records by supplying a relational expression in the CPYF command.

The program in Figure 9.8 illustrates how to use the CPYF command for file processing purposes.

9.3.2. Other Commands That Copy Data

Besides the CPYF command, there are several other copy file commands on the AS/400 that offer copy functions that have the same functionality but for different file types. They include:

- Copy From Tape (CPYFRMTAP)
- Copy To Tape (CPYTOTAP)
- Copy From Diskette (CPYFRMDKT)

```
SEQNBR* ...+... 1 ...+... 2 ...+... 3 ...+... 4 ...+... 5 ...+... 6 ...+... 7 ...+...
  100              PGM
  200              ALCOBJ     OBJ((DEMO/FILE1 *FILE *EXCL)) WAIT(180)
  300              MONMSG     MSGID(CPF1002 CPF1085) EXEC(DO)
  400              CRTPF      FILE(FILE1) SRCFILE(*CURLIB/QDDSSRC) +
  500                           SRCMBR(*FILE) MBR(*FILE) MAXMBRS(*NOMAX) +
  600                           LVLCHK(*NO)
  700              OVRDBF     FILE(FILE1) TOFILE(*CURLIB/FILE1) +
  800                           MBR(*FIRST) LVLCHK(*NO)
  900              CRTLF      FILE(FILE2) SRCFILE(QDDSSRC) SRCMBR(FILE2) +
 1000                           OPTION(*NOLIST *NOSOURCE) LVLCHK(*NO)
 1100              OVRDBF     FILE(FILE2) TOFILE(*CURLIB/FILE2)
 1200              ENDDO
 1300              CALL       PGM(PGM1) PARM(FILE1)
 1400              CPYF       FROMFILE(FILE1) TOFILE(FILE3) FROMMBR(*FIRST)
 1500              ENDPGM

                   * * * * END OF SOURCE * * * *
```

Figure 9.8.

- Copy To Diskette (CPYTODKT)
- Copy Source File (CPYSRCF)

However, these commands are only applicable to from-files and to-files that match the file type as specified by these commands.

The program in Figure 9.9 illustrates how to implement the CPYTOTAP command in a CL program for file-to-tape copying purposes.

```
SEQNBR* ...+... 1 ...+... 2 ...+... 3 ...+... 4 ...+... 5 ...+... 6 ...+... 7 ...+...
  100              PGM
  200              DCL        VAR(&REPLY) TYPE(*CHAR) LEN(1)
  300              DCL        VAR(&WSID) TYPE(*CHAR) LEN(10)
  400              CHGJOB     SWS(00000000)
  500              RTVJOBA    JOB(&WSID)
  600              RMVMSG     MSGQ(&WSID) CLEAR(*ALL)
  700              SNDBRKMSG  MSG('Mount tape then press ENTER to continue +
  800                           or C to cancel...') TOMSGQ(&WSID) +
  900                           MSGTYPE(*INQ) RPYMSGQ(&WSID)
 1000              RCVMSG     MSGQ(&WSID) MSGTYPE(*RPY) WAIT(*MAX) MSG(&REPLY)
 1100              IF         COND(&REPLY *EQ 'C') THEN(DO)
 1200              GOTO       CMDLBL(EOJ)
 1300              ENDDO
 1400              IF         COND(&REPLY *EQ 'C') THEN(DO)
 1500              GOTO       CMDLBL(EOJ)
 1600              ENDDO
 1700              CPYTOTAP   FROMFILE(DEMO/FILE1) TOFILE(QTAPE) +
 1800                           TOSEQNBR(1) TODEV(QTAPE) +
 1900                           TORCDLEN(*FROMFILE) TOENDOPT(*LEAVE) +
 2000                           TOVOL(*NONE)
 2100              MONMSG     MSGID(CPF0000) EXEC(CHGJOB SWS(00000010))
 2200              IF         COND(%SWITCH(XXXXXX1X)) THEN(DO)
 2300              SNDBRKMSG  MSG('An error occurred during the CPYTOTAP +
 2400                           command') TOMSGQ(&WSID) MSGTYPE(*INFO)
 2500              GOTO       CMDLBL(EOJ)
 2600              ENDDO
 2700     EOJ:     ENDPGM

                   * * * * END OF SOURCE * * * *
```

Figure 9.9.

9.4. Dynamic Sorting and Selection

The Open Query File (OPNQRYF) command is the CL command that gives interactive query capability to HLL programs on the AS/400. The OPNQRYF command selects, sorts, and presents data to an HLL program in a manner specified by the user at program runtime. It can even create new fields and summarizes data and passes it to the HLL program for processing as well.

The OPNQRYF command creates a shareable open data path to the file through which data can be accessed by an HLL program. The HLL program would still open the database file as usual, but instead of using a file pointer created by itself, it would use the pointer created by the OPNQRYF command to access the data records in the queried database file. Since we can select and sort the records the way we want in the OPNQRYF command, the HLL program only processes those records that meet the conditions specified in the OPNQRYF command.

Tip

OPNQRYF produces an open data path but not an output file.

Functions provided by the OPNQRYF command include the following:

- Dynamic record selection
- Dynamic keyed access paths
- Dynamic join functions
- Unique key processing
- Mapped field definitions
- Group and final total processing
- Optimization options

Generally speaking, the OPNQRYF command can select and sort data records faster and with more efficiency than the HLL programs since the record selection process is done in microcode. The OPNQRYF command filters the records from the database file and passes them to the HLL program for processing. Therefore, we may say that the OPNQRYF is very similar to access path in terms of functionality. However, the open data path created by the OPNQRYF command only lasts for the duration of the job, but the logical files are permanent objects stored in libraries; thus, using OPNQRYF means less overhead.

The syntax of the OPNQRYF command is quite complex, but we only need to specify the most basic ones in most situations. The following syntax includes the most basic requirements of the OPNQRYF command:

```
OPNQRYF FILE(file-names) QRYSLT('logical-expression') +
  KEYFLD(key-field-names)
```

In most situations, you only need to specify the FILE, QRYSLT (query select), and KEYFLD (key fields) parameters.

The QRYSLT (query select) parameter filters the records of the database file and passes them to the HLL program for processing. This is the parameter that determines which records to include in the open data path created by OPNQRYF. Of course, you can select records from the database file in your HLL program; however, the query processor is more efficient and faster. The value of the QRYSLT parameter is a character string containing the logical expression. The logical expression can contain any field names of the database files, operators, parentheses, constants, and built-in functions. The OPNQRYF command interprets the expression at program runtime, and each record in the database file is examined against the selection criteria; if the record satisfies the criteria, it is passed to the HLL program.

You can implement dynamic record selection by including the following in the QRYSLT parameter:

1. Variable
   ```
   QRYSLT('DATE *EQ &DAT')
   ```
   , where &DAT is a CL variable
2. Range of values
   ```
   QRYSLT('DATE *EQ %RANGE("930101" "930630")')
   ```
3. The CONTAIN (*CT) function
   ```
   QRYSLT('ADDRESS *CT "Highway 6" ')
   ```
4. Logical operators, e.g.,
   ```
   QRYSLT('AMOUNT *EQ 0 *AND DATE *LE "930701" ')
   ```
5. Field conversion using the MAPFLD parameter
6. The wildcard (*WLDCRD) function
   ```
   QRYSLT('DATE *EQ %WLDCRD("93__01") ')
   ```
   etc.

The KEYFLD parameter sorts the records before it passes them to the HLL program for processing. Also the KEYFLD parameter allows the random access of the database file. You can hard-code a group of field names in this parameter, and at the same time you can specify program variables in this parameter. This provides greater flexibility in design because it allows the user to choose the key fields at program runtime. This is the way OPNQRYF sorts the records and presents them to the HLL program for processing. Key fields specified in this parameter can be in ascending or descending order.

The steps to implement the OPNQRYF command in our CL programs include the following:

Step 1.   Override the database file to SHARE(*YES); the purpose is to ensure that the open data path created by OPNQRYF is shared by all "opens" of the same member in the same job.

Step 2.   Determine the key fields and the selection criteria for the records of the queried file, and code these criteria in the OPNQRYF command.

Step 3.   Call the HLL program; now the HLL program will process the open data path created by OPNQRYF instead of the file itself.

Step 4.   Use the CLOF command to close the query file after the HLL program is finished; this also gets rid of the open data path. Note that the access path created by the OPNQRYF command remains open until it is explicitly closed. The access path is maintained as an *IMMED access path; therefore it is very important that it is closed after the HLL is done.

Step 5.   Delete the override to the database file.

OPNQRYF requires the HLL program it calls to access the data records using the open data path that it created. Unless the database file is already open and the share open data path attribute in the file descriptions is *YES, we need to override the file with the share open data path parameter set to *YES. We always want to implement an OVRDBF in our CL programs for this purpose.

In the HLL program that we call in the CL program, the file name must match the value in the FORMAT parameter of the OPNQRYF command. If there is only one file specified in the FILE parameter of the OPNQRYF command, the FORMAT parameter would default to the file name specified. In the HLL program, you can specify whether the file will be accessed by key or processed sequentially. However, if your OPNQRYF command has created a keyed open data path and your HLL program processes the records sequentially, your program will receive a system-level error message

(message identifier CPF4123). Therefore, you should try to be more consistent in both the OPNQRYF command and the HLL program.

The OPNQRYF command works best over an existing access path. Also, record selection can be enhanced if an existing access path is keyed by the fields that record selection is based upon.

The program in Figure 9.10 illustrates the implementation of the OPNQRYF command.

```
SEQNBR* ...+... 1 ...+... 2 ...+... 3 ...+... 4 ...+... 5 ...+... 6 ...+... 7 ...+...
  100  PGM
  200           DCL      VAR(&FROMDATE) TYPE(*CHAR) LEN(4)
  300           DCL      VAR(&TODATE) TYPE(*CHAR) LEN(4)
  400           DCL      VAR(&SORTTYPE) TYPE(*CHAR) LEN(1)
  500           DCL      VAR(&DFTOUTQ) TYPE(*CHAR) LEN(10)
  600           DCL      VAR(&LIB) TYPE(*CHAR) LEN(10) VALUE(DEMO)
  700           DCL      VAR(&MSG) TYPE(*CHAR) LEN(132)
  800           DCL      VAR(&MSGID) TYPE(*CHAR) LEN(7)
  900           DCL      VAR(&MSGDTA) TYPE(*CHAR) LEN(128)
 1000           MONMSG   MSGID(CPF0000) EXEC(GOTO CMDLBL(ERROR))
 1100           CRTDUPPBJ   OBJ(FILE01) FROMLIB(&LIB) OBJTYPE(*FILE) +
 1200                       TOLIB(QTEMP) DATA(*NO)
 1300           CHGVAR   VAR(&FROMDATE) VALUE(%SST(*LDA 2 4))
 1400           CHGVAR   VAR(&TODATE) VALUE(%SST(*LDA 6 4))
 1500           CHGVAR   VAR(&SORTTYPE) VALUE(%SST(*LDA 10 1))
 1600           CPYF     FROMFILE(DEMO/DATA1) TOFILE(QTEMP/FILE01) +
 1700                    FROMMBR(*FIRST) TOMBR(*FROMMBR) +
 1800                    MBROPT(*ADD) FMTOPT(*MAP *DROP)
 1900           OVRDBF   FILE(FILE1) TOFILE(QTEMP/FILE1) SHARE(*YES) +
 2000                    /* override the file with attribute +
 2100                    share(*yes) */
 2200           OPNQRYF  FILE((QTEMP/FILE1)) FORMAT(FILE1) +
 2300                    KEYFLD((RECTYP) (TYPNUM) (REV13 +
 2400                    *DESCEND)) OPTIMIZE(*FIRSTIO)
 2500           CALL     PGM(PGM01) /* PGM01 is the HLL program */
 2600           CLOF     OPNID(FILE1)
 2700           DLTOVR   FILE(FILE01)
 2800  ERROR:
 2900           RCVMSG   RMB(*NO) MSG(&MSG) MSGDTA(&MSGDTA) +
 3000                    MSGID(&MSGID)
 3100           IF       COND(&MSG *NE ' ') THEN(DO)
 3200           IF       COND(%SST(&MSGID 1 3) *NE 'CPF') THEN(DO)
 3300           SNDPGMMSG MSG(&MSG) MSGTYPE(*DIAG)
 3400           ENDDO
 3500           ELSE     CMD(DO)
 3600           SNDPGMMSG MSGID(&MSGID) MSGF(QCPFMSG) MSGDTA(&MSGDTA) +
 3700                    MSGTYPE(*DIAG)
 3800           ENDDO
 3900           GOTO     CMDLBL(ERROR)
 4000           ENDDO
 4100           SNDPGMMSG MSG('program ended Abnormally.') MSGTYPE(*DIAG)
 4200           CHGJOB   LOG(4 00 *SECLVL) LOGCLPGM(*YES)
 4300           ENDPGM
```

Figure 9.10.

9.5. Spooled File

9.5.1. What Is Spooling?

The spooling function on the AS/400 allows the output files of the batch job to be sent to disk storage instead of being sent to the printers or any other output devices directly, and this allows the batch job to be independent of the print job, which may be a lot slower than the batch job itself depending on the availability and the speed of the printers or any other output devices.

Figure 9.11 shows the whole spooling function and the elements in the spooling process.

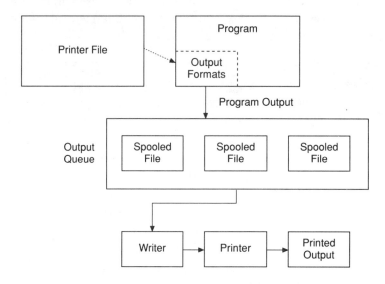

Figure 9.11. The spooled file and spooling function.

The printer file is a type of device file that determines how the output file would look and how the output function would perform. The printer file definitions are coded either as an externally described file or a program-described file, and will be copied into the program when the HLL program is compiled. The program controls the output formats. The output of the program will be written to spooled files according to the formats determined in the printer file. The spooled files will be stored on disk storage until they are printed or deleted. The writer controls the operations of the output devices, for example, a printer, and the spooled files are printed through the printer.

9.5.2. Commands That Work with Spooled Files

There is a set of system commands that allows you to work with the spooled files. The Work with Spooled Files (WRKSPLF) command allows you to display a list of spooled files associated with a user profile or print device:

```
WRKSPLF
```

The Change Spooled File Attributes (CHGSPLFA) command allows you to change some of the attributes of the spooled files, for example, the printer name, print sequence, number of copies, output queue, whether to save the file on disk after printing, output priority, and so forth.

The Copy Spooled File (CPYSPLF) command copies a spooled file into a database file.

In the spooled file commands that we have come across above, we would always need to supply the spooled file name as the required parameter of the commands. Most of the time, the spooled file name is just the name of the job that produced the spooled files, unless the output file name is explicitly specified in the program. Each spooled file also has a spooled file number associated with it; this is done because more than one spooled file can be produced by the same program in the same job, and the spooled file number can be used in combination with the spooled file name to identify among them. When we display the list of spooled files, we may see several spooled files produced by the same program in the same job (for example, DSP01/USER1/123456). In order to identify any particular spooled file in this situation, we need to make use of the spooled file number.

Command Summary

DSPFD	Display File Descriptions
CRTPF	Create a Physical File
ADDPFM	Add Physical File Member
CRTLF	Create a Logical File
DSPDBR	Display Database Relations
CLRPFM	Clear Physical File Member
CHGPF	Change Physical File
CHGPFM	Change Physical File Member
DSPPFM	Display Physical File Member
RGZPFM	Reorganize Physical File Member
RNMM	Rename Member
RMVM	Remove Member

DLTF	Delete a File
RCVF	Receive File
SNDF	Send File
SNDRCVF	Send/Receive File
OVRDBF	Override Database File
CPYF	Copy File
OPNQRYF	Open Query File
WRKSPLF	Work with Spooled Files
CPYSPLF	Copy Spooled File
CHGSPLFA	Change Spooled File Attributes

Exercises

9.1. What commands can be used to create a physical file? A logical file?

9.2. What is a member of a file?

9.3. What is an open data path?

9.4. Explain the function of the following commands:
- SNDF
- RCVF
- SNDRCVF

9.5. Explain the different functions of the OVRDBF command.

9.6. What are the main steps in using the OPNQRYF command?

9.7. What is the purpose of file spooling?

10

Advanced Topics

10.1. User-written Commands

There are over 700 CL commands provided by AS/400 to do a wide variety of system tasks on the system. However, as time goes by, you may find that the commands provided by the operating system may not be able to meet all your needs and accomplish all your tasks. In these situations, you may want to write commands and programs that are tailor-made to meet your own specific needs. These kind of commands and programs are called user-written command programs.

The main steps to create your own command are as follows:

1. Create the command definition statements.
2. Create the command definition objects, which include the command processing program (CPP), validity checking program (optional), and prompt control program (optional).
3. Compile the command definition statements using the create command (CRTCMD).

10.1.1. Components of the Command Definition Statements

The command definition statements of your user-written command are stored in a source physical file like other HLL programs and Data Description Specifications. However, they have special statement keywords and syntax. A command source program would include the following statements:

1. Command statement (CMD)

    The command statement specifies the prompt text for the command name. There is an example command source program in Figure 10.1 later, where the prompt text for the user-written command DLTLF 'Delete Dependent Logicals' is specified in the CMD statement. This is the text you would see at the top of the command prompt screen. In every command source program, only one CMD statement is allowed.

2. Parameter statement (PARM)

    The parameter statements define the parameters for the command. In our example in Figure 10.1, there is only one parameter for the DLTLF command, that is, the physical file name. However, you can specify up to 75 parameters in any one command program. The order of the PARM statements in your command source program determines their order of appearance on the prompt screens. The parameters specified in the command definition statements are passed to the command processing program as parameters (we should remember that parameters are passed by their positions in the parameter list, as mentioned in Chapter 7). In our example, the name of the parameter keyword is called FILE for the DLTLF command, and the value that can be entered to the FILE parameter has data type as specified in the two qualifier statements below it. You are required to enter the first parameter of the command, as indicated by the MIN parameter.

    You can limit the range of values for the parameter using the RANGE keyword of the PARM statement. The command automatically checks the value for the parameter when it is entered. For example, if we want to limit the range of values between 1 and 12 for a parameter called MONTH, we can code this in the PARM statement:

```
PARM KWD(MONTH) +
     TYPE(*DEC) +
     LEN(2 0) +
     RANGE(1 12)+
     PROMPT('Processing Month')
```

You can also use the REL (Relationship) keyword to limit the values by the parameter's relationship to another parameter or a constant. For example, if the processing day must be greater than zero, you can code the PARM statement like this:

```
PARM KWD(DAY) +
    TYPE(*DEC) +
    LEN(2 0) +
    REL(*GT 0) +
    PROMPT('processing day')
```

If you want to compare the processing day with another parameter &START_DAY, and only accept a processing day which is greater than the starting day, you can code the PARM statement like this:

```
PARM KWD(DAY) +
    TYPE(*DEC) +
    LEN(2 0) +
    REL(*GT &START_DATE) +
    PROMPT('processing day')
```

Note that the starting day parameter should be preceded by an &.

You can also restrict the values the parameter can accept by specifying those acceptable values in the VALUES parameter. For example, if the parameter can only accept JAN, FEB, and MAR into the processing month parameter, code the PARM statement like this:

```
PARM KWD(MONTH) +
    TYPE(*CHAR) +
    LEN(3) +
    VALUES(JAN FEB MAR) +
    PROMPT('processing month')
```

When the VALUES parameter is used, only up to 30 characters of the parameter data will be displayed where the text is displayed.

3. Element statement (ELEM)

The element statements define the element in a list used as parameter values. In our example, we do not have the list for the FILE parameter values since we want the user to supply the file and library names themselves and we cannot know what file and library names the user would enter for this parameter; thus we would not have the list of valid file and library names for the FILE parameter in advance. In other situations, such as the parameter is the location, say, we would know that the location can be either "local" or "remote"; we can code the ELEM statement for the possible values for the location parameter. You can specify up to 300 ELEM statements in one command program.

4. Dependent statement (DEP)

   The dependent statements define the relationship among the parameters. In our example, there is only one parameter so there is no parameter relationship at all.

   However, when you want to prevent the user from entering a parameter greater then another parameter, you can code the DEP statement like this:

   ```
   PARM KWD(VAR1) +
        TYPE(*DEC) +
        LEN(5 2) +
        PROMPT('first value')
   PARM KWD(VAR2) +
        TYPE(*DEC) +
        LEN(5 2) +
        PROMPT('second value')
     DEP CTL(*ALWAYS) PARM(&VAR2 *GE &VAR1)
   ```

   Note that the parameters in the DEP statement are preceded by &.

   If you want an error message to be sent when the condition is violated, code the DEP statement like this:

   ```
   DEP  CTL(*ALWAYS)  PARM(&VAR2  *GE  &VAR1)
   MSGID(.........)
   ```

   Whenever a message description is referred to in the DEP statement as above, you need to specify the message file parameter when you compile the command.

5. Prompt Control statement (PMTCTL)

   The prompt control statement defines the prompting given for parameters, and controls whether the command processor will display a parameter on the prompt panel. In some cases, the need to enter a specific parameter totally depends on the value supplied to another parameter. When a parameter is optional or only has meaning when another parameter contains a certain value, you need the prompt control statement to control this situation.

For instance, the user has to specify the 'output format' for a command that displays the contents in an object. If the value entered for 'output format' is *OUTFILE, say, then the 'output file name' parameter is needed as well. On the contrary, if the value entered is *SCREEN, say, then there is no need to enter the 'output file name'. Therefore, the 'output file name' parameter is under prompt control and becomes meaningful only when the output format is *OUTFILE. In the command program, the PMTCTL statements are used to control which parameters would be prompted and under what conditions.

When you specify *NONE for the PMTCTL parameter, every parameter defined in a command source member is displayed. However, if you specify other than *NONE for the PMTCTL parameter, no more parameters appear unless the user presses a key.

For example, if you want the command to prompt for the state when the user specifies the country as USA, you can code the PARM statement like this:

```
PARM KWD(STATE) +
    TYPE(*CHAR) +
    LEN(10) +
    VALUES(*ALL TX NY CA) +
    PMTCTL(STATE) +
    PROMPT('State')
STATE: PMTCTL CTL(COUNTRY) COND((*EQ USA))
```

The PMTCTL value links the parameter to a prompt control statement with the label.

When you specify *PMTRQS for the PMTCTL parameter, the parameter will be displayed only when <F10> is pressed.

6. Qualifier statement (QUAL)

The qualified name is the name of an object preceded by the name of the library. If the parameter value in our command is a qualified name, we need to define the separate components in the qualified name using the QUAL statements. The qualifier statements define the qualifiers of the name used as a parameter. You can specify up to 300 qualifiers for a qualified name. The order of the QUAL statements in the program determines the order of the qualifiers being passed to the validity checking program and the command processing program. In our example, there are two qualifiers for the FILE parameter value. The first value is of data type *NAME, which is a character string of length 10, where the first character in the string must be alphabetic, $, #, or @. Expression is allowed for the parameter value. The second value is also of data type *NAME of length 10, with default value *LIBL. You can also enter an expression for the parameter value.

```
PARM KWD(OUTFILE) TYPE(QUAL1) +
    PMTCTL(OUTFILE) +
    PROMPT('output file name')
QUAL1: QUAL TYPE(*NAME) LEN(10)
       QUAL TYPE(*NAME) LEN(10) +
           DFT(*LIBL) +
           SPCVAL((*LIBL)) +
           PROMPT('library')
```

Figure 10.1 is the source program for the Delete Dependent Logicals (DLTLF) command.

```
/* The Delete Dependent Logicals Command lets you name a data base */
/*    file and delete all the dependent logicals.                   */
/*                                                                   */
/* The command name is DLTLF                                        */
              CMD          PROMPT('Delete Dependent Logicals')

              PARM         KWD(FILE) TYPE(QUAL1) MIN(1) +
                           PROMPT('Physical file name')
  QUAL1:      QUAL         TYPE(*NAME) LEN(10) EXPR(*YES)
              QUAL         TYPE(*NAME) LEN(10) DFT(*LIBL) SPCVAL(*LIBL) +
                           EXPR(*YES) PROMPT('Library name')
```

Figure 10.1. Delete Dependent Logicals (DLTLF) command source program.

When the user has entered all the necessary parameters for the command, the command program passes these parameters to the command processing program (CPP). The command processing program can be a CL program or any other HLL program that the command calls to perform the actions. The CL program in Figure 10.2 is the CPP for the DLTLF command.

```
            PGM          PARM(&FILENAME)
            DCLF         FILE(QADSPDBR) /* This is the output file +
                           name for the DSPDBR command */
            DCL          VAR(&FILENAME) TYPE(*CHAR) LEN(20)
            DCL          VAR(&FILE) TYPE(*CHAR) LEN(10)
            DCL          VAR(&LIB) TYPE(*CHAR) LEN(10)
            DCL          VAR(&ALCOBJ) TYPE(*CHAR) LEN(1)
            DCL          VAR(&ERRORSW) TYPE(*LGL) /* Std err */
            DCL          VAR(&MSGID) TYPE(*CHAR) LEN(7) /* Std err */
            DCL          VAR(&MSGDTA) TYPE(*CHAR) LEN(100) /* Std err */
            DCL          VAR(&MSGF) TYPE(*CHAR) LEN(10) /* Std err */
            DCL          VAR(&MSGFLIB) TYPE(*CHAR) LEN(10) /* Std err */
            MONMSG       MSGID(CPF0000) EXEC(GOTO CMDLBL)STDERR1)) /* +
                           Std err */
            CHGVAR       VAR(&FILE) VALUE(%SST(&FILENAME 1 10))
            CHGVAR       VAR(&LIB) VALUE(%SST(&FILENAME 11 10))
            CHKOBJ       OBJ(&LIB/&FILE) OBJTYPE(*FILE) /* see if the +
                           file specified exists */
            ALCOBJ       OBJ((&LIB/&FILE *FILE *EXCL)) WAIT(0) /* +
                           allocate the object at exclusive mode */
            MONMSG       MSGID(CPF0000) EXEC(DO)
            SNDPGMMSG    MSGID(CPF9898) MSGF(QCPFMSG) MSGDTA('Cannot +
                           allocate file at exclusive mode to allow +
                           delete') MSGTYPE(*ESCAPE)
            ENDDO
            CHGVAR       VAR(&ALCOBJ) VALUE('X')
            DSPDBR       FILE(&LIB/&FILE) OUTPUT(*OUTFILE) +
                           OUTFILE(QTEMP/DSPDBRP) /* display +
                           database file relations and write the +
                           output to a file */
            OVRDBF       FILE(QADSPDBR) TOFILE (QTEMP/DSPDBRP)
READ:       RCVF         /* read the output file of the DSPDBR +
                           command */
            MONMSG       MSGID(CPF0864) EXEC(GOTO CMDLBL (EOF))
            IF           COND(&WHREFI *EQ ' ') THEN(GOTO +
                           CMDLBL(NOFILES))
            DLTF         FILE(&WHRELI/&WHREFI) /* delete the logical +
                           file */
            SNDPGMMSG    MSG('File ' *CAT & WHREFI *TCAT ' in ' *CAT +
                           &WHRELI *TCAT ' deleted') /* send a +
                           message that the logical file is deleted. */
            GOTO         CMDLBL(READ) /* read next output file record */
NOFILES:
            SNDPGMMSG    MSG('no logical files depend on the physical +
                           file') MSGTYPE(*COMP)
            GOTO         CMDLBL(ENDPGM)
EOF:        SNDPGMMSG    MSG('All dependent files deleted for ' *CAT +
                           &FILE *TCAT ' in' *CAT &WHRLI) +
                           MSGTYPE(*COMP) /* send a completion +
                           message by the end of the job */
ENDPGM:
            DLCOBJ       OBJ99&LIB/&FILE *FILE *EXCL))
            RETURN
STDERR1:
            IF           COND(&ERRORSW) THEN(SNDPGMMSG MSGID(CPF9999) +
                           MSGF(QCPFMSG) MSGTYPE(*ESCAPE)) /* +
                           function check error */
            CHGVAR       VAR(&ERRORSW) VALUE('1')
STDERR2:    RCVMSG       MSGTYPE(*DIAG) MSGDTA(&MSGDTA) MSGID(&MSGID) +
            IF             MSGF(&MSGF) MSGFLIB(&MSGFLIB)
                         COND(&MSGID *EQ ' ') THEN(GOTO +
            SNDPGMMSG      CMDLBL(STDERR3))
                         MSGID(&MSGID) MSGF(&MSGFLIB/&MSGF) +
            GOTO           MSGDTA(&MSGDTA) MSGTYPE(*DIAG)
STDERR3:    RCVMSG       CMDLBL(STDERR2)
                         MSGTYPE(*EXCP) MSGDTA(&MSGDTA) MSGID(&MSGID) +
            DLCOBJ         MSGF(&MSGF) MSGFLIB(&MSGFLIB)
            MONMSG         OBJ((&LIB/&FILE *FILE *EXCL))
            SNDPGMMSG    MSGID(CPF1005)
                         MSGID(&MSGID) MSGF(&MSGFLIB/&MSGF) +
            ENDPGM         MSGDTA(&MSGDTA) MSGTYPE(*ESCAPE)
```

10.1.2. How Commands Are Created

User-written command source code is compiled and created by the Create Command (CRTCMD) command. Figure 10.3 is the prompt screen for the CRTCMD command. Enter the name for the user-written command and the name of the CPP program in the 'Program to process command' parameter.

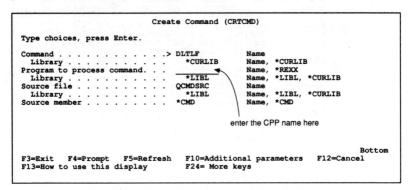

```
                         Create Command (CRTCMD)

 Type choices, press Enter.

 Command . . . . . . . . . . . .> DLTLF        Name
   Library . . . . . . . . . . .    *CURLIB     Name, *CURLIB
 Program to process command. . .                Name, *REXX
   Library . . . . . . . . . . .    *LIBL       Name, *LIBL, *CURLIB
 Source file . . . . . . . . . .   QCMDSRC      Name
   Library . . . . . . . . . . .    *LIBL       Name, *LIBL, *CURLIB
 Source member . . . . . . . . .    *CMD        Name, *CMD

                                      enter the CPP name here


                                                                   Bottom
 F3=Exit    F4=Prompt   F5=Refresh   F10=Additional parameters  F12=Cancel
 F13=How to use this display         F24= More keys
```

Figure 10.3.

You can restrict a command to run only in batch mode or interactive mode by specifying *BPGM or *IPGM in the ALLOW parameter in the CRTCMD command.

After you have compiled the command and the CPP successfully, you can run your command at the system command line like any other system commands. Type in the command name DLTLF and press <F4>; the prompt screen will come up as shown in Figure 10.4.

```
                     Delete Dependent Logicals (DLTLF)

 Type choices, press Enter.

 Physical file name . . . . . . .                  Name
   Library name . . . . . . . . .   *LIBL          Name, *LIBL








                                                                   Bottom
 F3=Exit    F4=Prompt   F5=Refresh   F12=Cancel   F13=How to use this display
 F24=More keys
```

Figure 10.4.

10.2. System Functions and API

There are a group of system programs that you can call from within your CL or HLL programs. These programs are collectively called Application Programming Interface (API) and provide a vehicle for communication between the user-written program and the operating system and other system objects. Broadly speaking, APIs are system programs that provide access to specific data or functions in the system domain; they allow the programmers to access low-level machine functions or system data from within an HLL program. Generally speaking, calling an API program is more efficient and faster than calling a CL command in your HLL program. In the program in Figure 10.5, we have used the API programs called QCMDCHK and QCMDEXC. The QCMDCHK program can be called from within a CL program; the function of this system program is to check the syntax of the specified character string passed as a parameter and see if it is a valid command statement with all the required parameter values specified. You can call the QCMDCHK program with the following syntax in your program:

```
CALL PGM(QCMDCHK) PARM(&string &length)
```

```
            PGM             /* This program illustrates the purpose of +
                               the system functions QCMDCHK and QCMDEXC */
            DCL             VAR(&STRING) TYPE(*CHAR) LEN(30)
            DCL             VAR(&LENGTH) TYPE(*DEC) LEN(15 5) VALUE(30)
            .
            .
            .
            CHGVAR          VAR(&STRING) VALUE('user-command-string')
            .
            .
            .
            CALL            PGM(QCMDCHK) PARM(&STRING &LENGTH) /* +
                               QCMDCHK would interpret the character +
                               string contained in &STRING and check if +
                               there is any syntax error in it. */
            MONMSG          MSGID(CPF0006) EXEC(GOTO CMDLBL(EXIT))
            .
            .
            .
            CALL            PGM(QCMDEXC) PARM(&STRING &LENGTH) /* +
                               QCMDEXC would interpret the character +
                               string contained in &STRING and run it as +
                               if it is a command */
            MONMSG          MSGID(CPF0006) EXE(SNDPGMMSG MSG('user +
                               input command string has syntax error +
                               while system tried to execute it'))
            .
            .
            .
EXIT:       ENDPGM
```

Figure 10.5. Program using QCMDCHK and QCMDEXC.

The &string parameter is a character string containing the command statement to be checked or prompted. The &length parameter specifies the maximum length of the character string to be passed to the QCMDCHK program. Then the QCMDCHK program checks the syntax of the command statement contained in the character string, and the required parameters of the command. However, it does not check the running environment that is required to run the command. If a syntax error is found by the QCMDCHK program, then the QCMDCHK function will send an escape message to the program. You can monitor the error message using the MONMSG command. You can also request prompting for the parameters by using the selective prompt character (covered in the next section) in the command statement contained in the character string. This will allow the prompt screen of the command to be displayed so that the user can supply the values for the parameter at program runtime. If there is no error found by the QCMDCHK program, the command string is placed back in the variable that contained the character string. The QCMDEXC program is called from within your HLL program in the following syntax:

```
CALL PGM(QCMDEXC) PARM(&string &length)
```

This program is called by any HLL program to interpret the command statement contained in the character string and run it as a valid command. The command statement that you want to run is contained in the character string variable &string in the above syntax, with its maximum length specified in the &length variable. After the command statement is run, control is returned to the HLL program. However, not all commands that passed the test of the QCMDCHK program would be run by the QCMDEXC program, since the syntax checking performed by the QCMDCHK program does not check the environment in which the command is allowed to run. If an error occurs when the command is executed by the QCMDEXC program, then an escape message is sent to the program, but of course you can monitor these error messages by the MONMSG command.

The table in Figure 10.6 lists the API programs provided by the operating system. These system programs are not difficult to use; for example, if you want a system command line to appear in a pop-up window when a certain function key is pressed in your program, you can simply call the QUSCMDLN program from within your HLL program.

```
API                 Function
--------            ----------------------------------------

QCMDCHK             check the syntax of a command string
QCMDEXC             execute a command string
QCLSCAN             scan for a string pattern
QSNDDTAQ            send an entry to a data queue
QRCVDTAQ            receive an entry from a data queue
QTBXLATE            translate a character according to a
                    translation table

QUSLMBR             list database file members
QDBLDBR             list database relations
QUSLRCD             list record formats
QDBRTVFD            retrieve file description

QMHRCVPM            receive program message
QMHRTVM             retrieve message
QMHSNDBM            send break message
QMHSNDPM            send program message

QSYCUSRA            check user authority to an object
QSYLAUTU            list authorized users
QSYLOBJA            list objects user is authorized to or
                    owns
QSYLUSRA            list users authorized to object

QUSCMDLN            display command line window
QUSCRTUS            create user space
QUSRTVUS            retrieve from user space
QUSCHGUS            change the contents in a user space

QUSLJOB             list job
QWDRJOBD            retrieve job description information
QUSRJOBI            retrieve job information
QWCCVTDT            convert date and time format
```

Figure 10.6. API programs.

For details of these API functions, please refer to the IBM System Programmer Interface Reference. You will need to supply the parameters of these functions in your program, and this reference manual gives you more information about them.

These API programs belong in the user domain but operate in the system state; they can be called by user-written programs to access the system domain objects. Remember that security level 40 imposes security to the system objects, so user-written programs can hardly access the information in these system objects if authority is not granted to these programs. However, by using API programs we are provided with a gateway to the AS/400 system internals.

10.3. Selective Prompting

As mentioned in Section 10.2, we can prompt the user to enter the parameter values for the command statement in the character string before it is passed to the QCMDCHK program for syntax checking. The advantage of this is that we may not be able to know which command will be checked and what parameters will be used when the command is created; selective prompting provides the capability that the user can make changes to the parameter values at program runtime.

You can request interactive prompting by placing the Selective Prompting character before the command statement. The Selective Prompting characters are listed in the table in Figure 10.7.

Selective Prompting Character	Function
??	the parameter is displayed and input-capable
?*	the parameter is displayed but not input-capable
?<	the parameter is displayed and is input-capable with the command default set to the CPP unless changed by the user
?/	reserved by IBM
?-	the parameter is not displayed and the default value is passed to the CPP

Figure 10.7. Selective Prompting characters.

As an example, say you want to implement an OVRDBF command in your CL program; you know which file you want to override, but you do not know which file is the overriding file and the member name when you compile the command. In this situation, you can place the ?? character to precede the TOFILE and MBR parameters, so that the user will be prompted with the OVRDBF display screen, and the user will determine the values for these parameters at runtime. The FILE parameter, on the other hand, is already determined and any changes to this parameter should not be allowed. Therefore we can place the ?* character to precede it so that this parameter is not input-capable in the prompt screen.

Figures 10.8 and 10.9 illustrate how we can combine selective prompting with API functions in our program.

Let's say we want to implement the command entry line on our display menu; the user can type the command needed to run and can press the Prompt key <F4> to enter the parameters. How can we do this?

```
R PROMPT
                                     CF04(94 'PROMPT')
    CMD             153A  B 20   1
                                     CHECK(LC)

                        .
                        .
                        .
                        .
                        .
```

Figure 10.8.

```
            PGM
            DCLF        FILE(SCREEN) RCDFMT(PROMPT)
            DCL         VAR(&CMD) TYPE(*CHAR) LEN(153)
            DCL         VAR(&CMD2) TYPE(*CHAR) LEN(512)
            .
            .
PROMPT:     SNDRCVF     RCDFMT(PROMPT)
            CHGVAR      VAR(&CMD2) VALUE(&CMD)
            .
            .
            IF          COND(&IN94 *EQ '1') THEN(DO)
            CHGVAR      VAR(&CMD2) VALUE('?' *CAT &CMD)
            CALL        PGM(QCMDEXC) PARM(&CMD2 512)
            GOTO        CMDLBL(PROMPT)
            ENDDO
            .
            .
            .

            CALL        PGM(QCMDEXC) PARM(&CMD2 512)
            ENDPGM
```

Figure 10.9.

We should have an input/output capable field in our display file definition. This field is called CMD, which is 153 characters long as shown in the display file definition in Figure 10.8.

Figure 10.9 is the CL program that receives the value of the variable &CMD, which is actually the command to run. When the Prompt key <F4> is pressed, the associated indicator 94 is set on and the character string contained in &CMD is preceded by the selective prompting character '?'. This character string will then be passed to the system function QCMDEXC for execution.

Index

Symbols

D

system values
  displaying, 23, 82
  QSYSLIBL, 82, 84
  QUSRLIBL, 82, 84
System/3, 2
  96-column card format, 2
  batch processing, 3
  Communications Control Program (CCP), 3
  memory, 2
  Operator Control Language (OCL), 3
  System Control Program (SCP), 3
System/32, 3
  memory, 3
System/34, 4
  Control Storage Processor (CSP), 4
  Main Storage Processor (MSP), 4
  memory, 4
System/36, 4
  dynamic random access memory (DRAM), 4
System/38, 4–5
  Control Program Facility (CPF), 5
  "logical" computer, 5
  object-based architecture, 5
  single-level addressability of storage, 4

T

temporary library, 73
temporary message queue, 139, 160–161
  external message queue, 160
  program message queue, 161
temporary objects, 73
terms and concepts, 16–19
  control language, 16–17
  job queue, 19
  jobs, 18
  libraries, 18
  message queue, 19
  objects, 17
  output queue, 19
  subsystem, 19

test library, 72, 74
Text Description (TEXT) parameter, 116
TFRCTL command, 67, 133
Time Slice (TIMESLICE) parameter, 105
Token Ring local area network (LAN) adapter, 10
trailing concatenation operator (*TCAT or l<), 54
Transfer Job (TFRJOB) command, 111
  Request Data (RTGDTA) parameter, 112
tutorials, 19–31, 33
TYPE (data type) keyword, 40

U

unconditional branching, 64
unconditional control flow, 64–65
Update (*SHRUPD) mode, 92
User (USER) parameter, 102
user libraries, naming, 74
user profile, 20
user tasks commands, 21
user-written commands, 219–226
  command definition statements, 219–225
  creation, 226

V

VAL (Initial Value) keyword, 40
VAR (Variable) keyword, 39
variables, 37
  both length and initial value omitted, 41
  character, 40
  DCL command declaration rules, 40–42
  decimal, 40
  declaring, 39–42, 57
  location, 38
  logical, 40
  maximum length, 41
  name and declaration, 35–42